SAINSBURY'S
VEGETARIAN COOKERY
SARAH BROWN

SAINSBURY'S
VEGETARIAN COOKERY

SARAH BROWN

CONTENTS

INTRODUCTION	*5*
SOUPS	*6*
STARTERS	*24*
MAIN COURSES	*34*
LIGHT MAIN COURSES	*88*
SALADS	*98*
VEGETABLE ACCOMPANIMENTS	*116*
PUDDINGS	*122*
INDEX	*144*

CONTRIBUTING AUTHORS

Ian Burleigh

Roselyne Masselin

Christine Smith

Published exclusively for J Sainsbury plc,
Stamford House, Stamford Street, London SE1 9LL by
Dorling Kindersley Limited, 9 Henrietta Street,
London WC2E 8PS

First published 1988

Seventh impression 1991

Copyright © 1988 by Dorling Kindersley Limited,
London

Text copyright © 1988 by
Sarah Elizabeth Brown Limited

ISBN 0-86318-336-0

ACKNOWLEDGEMENTS

Designed by Bridgewater Design Limited

PHOTOGRAPHY
Martin Brigdale
Alan Duns
Graeme Harris
Graham Miller
Ian O'Leary
Charlie Stebbings
Clive Streeter

ILLUSTRATIONS: Lorraine Harrison

TYPESETTING: CST Limited, Hove

REPRODUCTION: Colourscan, Singapore

Printed and bound in Italy by L.E.G.O.

NOTES

■ Standard spoon measures are used in all recipes
■ 1 tablespoon = one 15 ml spoon
■ 1 teaspoon = one 5 ml spoon
■ All spoon measures are level.
■ Size 3 eggs should be used unless otherwise stated.
■ Prepare fresh chillis under running water and take care not to rub your
eyes while doing so. Wash your hands thoroughly afterwards.
■ To speed up preparation time, canned pulses can be used instead of dried
pulses. Pulses roughly double in weight when cooked so, for example, if a
recipe specifies 8 oz (250 g) dried pulses, you will need a 15 oz (432 g) can.
■ For all recipes, quantities are given in both metric and imperial measures.
Follow either set but not a mixture of both, because they are not
interchangeable.
■ Use freshly ground black pepper where pepper is specified.
■ Ovens should be preheated to the specified temperature.
■ If fresh herbs are unobtainable, use dried herbs instead but halve the
quantities stated.

*D*elicious, inexpensive and healthy, vegetarian dishes are easy to incorporate into the family repertoire as an interesting alternative to meat and fish. This book will, I hope, give you lots of ideas. It contains about 200 of my favourite recipes, including pasta and rice dishes, casseroles and bakes, pizzas and pancakes, plus a selection of starters, soups, salads and desserts.

Most of the recipes in this book require no special skill, and some of them certainly need not be a burden on your time. Some can be partly made in advance, then finished off at the last minute – ideal when you are entertaining.

High in fibre but low in fat, wholefoods form the basis of a vegetarian diet, and many of the ingredients used in this book will be familiar; any less familiar ones are illustrated so that you know exactly what to look for when you are shopping. I've included information on how to cook brown rice and wholemeal pasta as well as beans, nuts, lentils and dried fruit. Since all these ingredients keep for a long time, they provide a useful back-up in your store-cupboard and an excellent standby if you are confronted by unexpected guests.

A vegetarian diet also makes full use of fresh fruit and vegetables, both cooked and raw. A rich source of many essential vitamins and minerals, they add colour, texture and flavour to a meal. Their versatility lends interest to a diet, and many varieties are cheap, especially if you buy them in season. There's now a tremendous range of fruit and vegetables available, from the commonplace, but invaluable, carrots and onions and the familiar British orchard fruits to the exotic delights of the tropics. Fruit helps to satisfy a sweet tooth, so it may enable you to cut down on sugary foods. Don't confine it to a bowl on the sideboard; you'll find plenty of ideas in the book for using different varieties in sweet and savoury dishes.

Whether you want the occasional meatless meal or a completely vegetarian diet, you'll find many imaginative ideas in this book for dishes that are tasty and interesting yet simple to prepare.

Sarah Brown

▮ SOUPS ▮

PEANUT AND PAPRIKA SOUP	8
SPLIT PEA SOUP WITH BUTTERMILK	8
BUTTER BEAN AND HARICOT CHOWDER	8
SPICED CHICK PEA AND TOMATO SOUP	9
VERMICELLI CONSOMME	9
CONSOMME WITH FLORETS	9
CONSOMME JULIENNE	10
CHEESE AND PARSNIP SOUP WITH CARAWAY	10
ALMOND AND TOMATO SOUP	11
GREEN SPLIT PEA SOUP WITH CORIANDER	11
CREAMED ARTICHOKE SOUP	12
EASY PUMPKIN SOUP	12
WINTER VEGETABLE SOUP	13
AVOCADO AND LETTUCE SOUP	15
YOGURT AND TOMATO SOUP	15
CUCUMBER AND ORANGE SOUP	15
RASPBERRY AND ALMOND SOUP	17
GAZPACHO	17
BREAD STICKS (GRISSINI)	17
CRUSTY BREAD	18
GARLIC BREAD	18
CARAWAY SEED TOAST FINGERS	18
CHEESE RUSKS	18
HERB DUMPLINGS	19

FROM TOP: *Peanut and paprika soup (see p.8); Butter bean and haricot chowder (see p.8); Split pea soup with buttermilk (see p.8)*

PEANUT AND PAPRIKA SOUP

INGREDIENTS

- 2 tsp (10ml) groundnut or sunflower oil
- 1 onion, peeled and finely chopped
- 2 cloves garlic, crushed
- 1 red pepper, deseeded and finely chopped
- 4oz (125g) fennel bulb, diced
- 4oz (125g) smooth peanut butter
- 1 tsp (5ml) paprika
- ¼ tsp chilli powder
- 2–3 tbsp (30–45ml) apple juice
- juice of ½ a lemon
- 1 pint (600ml) vegetable stock
- salt and pepper

Illustrated on page 7

Peanuts are used in dips, sauces and soups in Indonesian and Far Eastern cuisines. They are a good source of protein and combine well with aromatic spices. Their flavour is complemented by the tang of lemon juice.

PREPARATION TIME: 15 mins
COOKING TIME: 40–45 mins
SERVES 4

METHOD

1 Heat the oil in a pan and gently fry the onion until soft and translucent. Add the garlic, red pepper and fennel. Cook for 3–5 minutes.
2 Stir in the remaining ingredients and mix thoroughly. Cook for 40–45 minutes, stirring frequently.
3 Season well and serve hot.

SPLIT PEA SOUP WITH BUTTERMILK

INGREDIENTS

- 2 tsp (10ml) sunflower oil
- 1 onion, peeled and finely chopped
- 1 clove garlic, crushed
- 2 sticks celery, trimmed and diced
- 4oz (125g) yellow split peas, rinsed
- 1 pint (600ml) vegetable stock
- 2 tbsp (30ml) tomato purée
- 1 tbsp (15ml) fresh dill
- ¼ pint (150ml) buttermilk
- salt and pepper

Illustrated on page 7

Split peas are ideal for soups; they need no soaking, cook quickly and, when puréed, they have a good creamy texture.

PREPARATION TIME: 20 mins
COOKING TIME: 40–45 mins for the peas
SERVES 4

METHOD

1 Heat the oil in a pan and fry the onion until soft and translucent. Add the garlic and celery and cook for 3–4 minutes.
2 Add the split peas and cook for 2 minutes. Pour over the vegetable stock, stir in the tomato purée and dill.
3 Cook for 40–45 minutes, or until the peas are quite soft.
4 Allow to cool, then purée in a blender or food processor, adding the buttermilk. Season well. Reheat gently before serving.

BUTTER BEAN AND HARICOT CHOWDER

INGREDIENTS

- 3oz (75g) mixed butter and haricot beans, soaked
- 1 tsp (5ml) olive oil
- 1 onion, peeled and finely chopped
- 8oz (250g) carrots, scrubbed and diced
- 1 green pepper, deseeded and diced
- ¼ tsp nutmeg
- 1 tsp (5ml) fennel seeds, crushed
- ½ tsp celery seeds or 2 sticks celery, finely chopped
- 2 fl oz (50ml) skimmed milk
- salt and pepper

Illustrated on page 7

This deliciously thick, nutritious soup is given a slight tang by the fennel, celery seeds and nutmeg. The beans give off a lovely aroma when cooking, while the carrots, onion and pepper provide a tasty and vitamin-rich base for the soup.

PREPARATION TIME: 15 mins (plus 10–12 hours soaking time)
COOKING TIME: 40–45 mins (plus 40–55 mins for the beans)
SERVES 4

METHOD

1 Drain the beans. Bring to the boil in plenty of fresh water. Boil fast for 10 minutes, then simmer for a further 35–45 minutes or until soft. Drain and reserve the stock.
2 Heat the oil in a pan and gently fry the onion. Add the carrots and pepper, cover the pan and soften for 10 minutes.
3 Purée 2oz (50g) of the beans with ½ pint (300ml) bean stock and the nutmeg. Add to the vegetables with the fennel and celery seeds or finely chopped celery.
4 Add the remaining beans and bring the soup to the boil, stirring occasionally. Cook for 40–45 minutes. Season well. Just before serving, add the milk, season and heat through.

Spiced chick pea and tomato soup

SPICED CHICK PEA AND TOMATO SOUP

INGREDIENTS

■ 2 tsp (10ml) olive oil
■ 1 onion, peeled and finely chopped
■ 2 cloves garlic
■ 1 tbsp (15ml) ground almonds
■ 2 tsp (10ml) garam masala
■ ½ tsp chilli powder
■ 1 tsp (5ml) ground coriander
■ 1 tsp (5ml) turmeric
■ 1 tsp (5ml) grated fresh root ginger
■ 14oz (400g) can tomatoes, puréed
■ 6oz (175g) cooked chick peas
■ ¾ pint (450ml) vegetable stock
■ salt and pepper

Illustrated above

If you wish to use dried chick peas, 3oz (75g) dry weight will make 6oz (175g) cooked. Soak them for 12 hours, drain and bring to the boil in plenty of unsalted water. Boil fast for 10 minutes, then cover and simmer for 40 minutes.
PREPARATION TIME: 15 mins
COOKING TIME: 35–45 mins
SERVES 4

METHOD

1 Heat the oil in a pan and gently fry the onion until soft and translucent. Add the crushed garlic and cook for 2 minutes.
2 Mix the ground almonds and spices with a little water to form a paste. Add this to the onions and cook for 2–3 minutes.
3 Stir in the tomatoes, chick peas and stock. Cook for 35–45 minutes so that the flavours develop. Season and serve hot.

VERMICELLI CONSOMME

INGREDIENTS

■ 1¼ pints (750ml) vegetable stock
■ 2 tsp (10ml) tomato purée
■ 2oz (50g) vermicelli
■ 1 red or green pepper, deseeded and diced
■ 1 carrot, peeled and diced
■ 1 tsp (5ml) green peppercorns, crushed
■ 1 tsp (5ml) chopped fresh chervil or parsley
■ salt and black pepper

Illustrated on page 10

This traditional Italian consommé is light, full of flavour and a little more substantial than vegetable-based consommés. Small pasta shapes could be substituted for vermicelli. Green peppercorns, the unripe berries of the familiar black peppercorns, are usually pickled in brine and add to the flavour.
PREPARATION TIME: 10 mins
COOKING TIME: 18 mins
SERVES 4

METHOD

1 Put the stock in a saucepan and bring to the boil. Add the tomato purée and vermicelli and simmer for a few seconds.
2 Stir in the pepper, carrot and peppercorns and simmer for 15 minutes.
3 Add the chopped chervil or parsley and season to taste. Serve hot.

CONSOMME WITH FLORETS

INGREDIENTS

■ 1½ pints (900ml) vegetable stock
■ 2oz (50g) peas
■ 2oz (50g) cauliflower florets, broken into small pieces
■ 2oz (50g) carrots, scrubbed and sliced
■ 2oz (50g) French beans, finely chopped
■ 1 bouquet garni
■ salt and black pepper

Illustrated on page 10

The bouquet garni gives a pervasive taste of herbs in this light and healthy consommé. If you grow your own herbs, you could make a bouquet garni by simply tying together a few sprigs of parsley, a sprig of thyme, a small bay leaf and any other herbs you like.
PREPARATION TIME: 5 mins
COOKING TIME: 15 mins
SERVES 4

METHOD

1 Place the stock in a saucepan and bring to the boil. Add the vegetables and the bouquet garni.
2 Simmer for 15 minutes or until the vegetables are tender.
3 Remove the bouquet garni, season to taste and serve hot.

FROM TOP: Vermicelli consommé (see p.9); Consommé with florets (see p.9); Consommé julienne

■ CONSOMME JULIENNE ■

INGREDIENTS

■ 2oz (50g) carrots, scrubbed
■ 2oz (50g) turnips, scrubbed
■ 2oz (50g) celery, trimmed
■ 2oz (50g) green cabbage
■ 1½ pints (900ml) vegetable stock
■ 1 bay leaf
■ salt and black pepper

Illustrated left

Consommé is a light clear soup which makes an excellent appetizer before a large main course. It is very light and full of flavour and contains many valuable nutrients. The vegetables, when cut into julienne strips, look attractive and provide texture.

PREPARATION TIME: 10 mins
COOKING TIME: 15 mins
SERVES 4

METHOD

1 Cut the vegetables into julienne (long, thin) strips.
2 Place the stock in a saucepan and bring to the boil. Add the vegetables and bay leaf and simmer for 10–15 minutes or until the vegetables are just tender.
3 Remove the bay leaf, season to taste and serve immediately.

■ CHEESE AND PARSNIP ■ SOUP WITH CARAWAY ■

INGREDIENTS

■ ½oz (15g) butter or margarine
■ 1 small onion, peeled and chopped
■ 1 tsp (5ml) caraway seeds
■ 3oz (75g) fennel, chopped
■ 2oz (50g) potatoes, scrubbed and diced
■ 10oz (300g) parsnips, cubed
■ 1¼ pints (750ml) stock or water
■ 2oz (50g) Cheddar cheese, grated
■ salt and black pepper

GARNISH

■ caraway seeds or a little grated cheese

Illustrated on page 11

Choose small or medium parsnips, avoiding any with dark patches.

PREPARATION TIME: 20 mins
COOKING TIME: 30 mins
SERVES 4

METHOD

1 Heat the butter in a saucepan and gently fry the onion with the caraway seeds until the onion is soft. Add the fennel and potatoes, and fry for a further 2–3 minutes.
2 Add the parsnips to the pan and fry for 1–2 minutes. Stir in the stock, bring to the boil, cover and simmer for 20–25 minutes. Cool slightly. Purée in a blender or food processor until smooth.
3 Reheat gently in a clean saucepan and bring to boiling point. Add the grated cheese and seasoning, stirring until the cheese has melted. Garnish with caraway seeds or cheese, and serve hot.

ALMOND AND TOMATO SOUP

INGREDIENTS

- 1 pint (600ml) water
- 6 large ripe tomatoes, chopped
- 2 bay leaves
- 2 tsp (10ml) paprika
- 4oz (125g) almonds, blanched

GARNISH
- toasted flaked almonds

Illustrated right

This orange-pink soup makes a colourful display on a dinner table.

PREPARATION TIME: 30 mins
COOKING TIME: 20 mins
SERVES 4

METHOD

1 Simmer the water, tomatoes and bay leaves for 15 minutes. Add the paprika and cook for 5 minutes. Leave to cool.
2 Meanwhile toast the almonds under a preheated grill until golden on both sides. Allow them to cool and then grind to a very fine powder or paste, keeping some whole for use as a garnish.
3 Purée the tomato mixture and the almonds together in a blender or food processor. Pour into a clean saucepan and reheat without boiling. Serve hot, garnished with almonds.

GREEN SPLIT PEA SOUP WITH CORIANDER

INGREDIENTS

- 1 tbsp (15ml) sunflower oil
- 1 onion, peeled and chopped
- 1 tsp (5ml) coriander seeds
- 1 clove garlic, crushed
- 2 sticks celery, chopped
- 8oz (250g) green split peas
- 1½ pints (900ml) vegetable stock
- 6oz (175g) mangetout peas
- ½oz (15g) coarsely chopped fresh coriander
- 2 tsp (10ml) soya sauce
- salt and black pepper

Illustrated right

Coriander quickly loses its flavour in water, so do not boil the soup after adding it.

PREPARATION TIME: 25 mins
COOKING TIME: about 1 hour
SERVES 4

METHOD

1 Heat the oil in a heavy-based saucepan and fry the onion and the coriander seeds until the onion is soft. Add the garlic and celery and fry for a further 5 minutes.
2 Rinse the split peas. Add them to the pan and cook over a low heat for 2–3 minutes, stirring all the time. Pour in the stock, bring to the boil and simmer for 40 minutes or until the peas start disintegrating. Add the mangetout peas and cook for a further 15 minutes.
3 Stir in the coriander, soya sauce and seasoning. Reheat gently, but do not boil. Serve immediately.

FROM TOP: Cheese and parsnip soup with caraway; Green split pea soup with coriander; Almond and tomato soup

CREAMED ARTICHOKE SOUP

INGREDIENTS

- 12oz (375g) Jerusalem artichokes
- 1 tsp (5ml) margarine or sunflower oil
- 1 small onion, peeled and chopped
- 4 sticks celery, trimmed and chopped
- 2 tsp (10ml) grated fresh root ginger
- 1½ pints (900ml) vegetable stock
- 1 bouquet garni

GARNISH
- 4 small gherkins, chopped or sliced

Illustrated right

Jerusalem artichokes are rather time-consuming to peel but have a nutty flavour which goes well with ginger.

PREPARATION TIME: 20 mins
COOKING TIME: 30 mins
SERVES 4

METHOD

1 Peel and chop the artichokes.
2 Melt the margarine in a saucepan and gently cook the onion, celery, ginger and Jerusalem artichokes for 1–2 minutes.
3 Add the stock and bouquet garni. Cover and simmer for 20–25 minutes or until the Jerusalem artichokes are tender. Allow to cool slightly. Remove the bouquet garni.
4 Purée in a blender or food processor until smooth. Pour the soup into a clean saucepan, season and reheat. Serve hot, garnished with the gherkins.

EASY PUMPKIN SOUP

INGREDIENTS

- 2lb (1kg) ripe orange pumpkin, outer skin and non-orange parts removed
- 4 fl oz (125ml) water
- 1½ pints (900ml) semi-skimmed milk
- salt and white pepper
- 1 tsp (5ml) honey (optional)

Illustrated right

Served with thick slices of wholemeal bread, this soup makes a delicious and satisfying supper dish on a cold evening.

PREPARATION TIME: 10 mins
COOKING TIME: 30 mins
SERVES 4

METHOD

1 Scoop out the pumpkin and set the seeds on one side. Dice the orange pumpkin flesh and put in a saucepan with the water. Simmer for about 15 minutes until soft.
2 Mash until smooth. Add the milk, bring to the boil and simmer for 5 minutes. Season to taste and add honey if liked.
3 Meanwhile, wash and toast the pumpkin seeds in a preheated oven at Gas Mark 5, 375°F, 190°C until crisp and brown. Serve the soup with croûtons or crusty bread (see page 18) and pumpkin seeds as a side snack.

FROM TOP: Creamed artichoke soup; Easy pumpkin soup

Winter vegetable soup

WINTER VEGETABLE SOUP

INGREDIENTS

- 1 tbsp (15ml) sunflower oil
- 4oz (125g) onion, peeled and chopped
- 2 tsp (10ml) fresh sage
- 2 tsp (10ml) fresh rosemary
- 1 bay leaf
- 2oz (50g) swede, scrubbed and diced
- 2oz (50g) turnip, scrubbed and diced
- 2oz (50g) mooli (Japanese radish), cut into strips
- 4oz (125g) carrots, scrubbed and diced
- 4oz (125g) green cabbage, chopped
- 1¾ pints (1 litre) stock or water
- 1 vegetable stock cube
- salt and black pepper

Illustrated above

A selection of inexpensive winter vegetables makes a warming, chunky soup for cold days. Other root vegetables and herbs can be substituted, according to preference and availability.

PREPARATION TIME: 15 mins
COOKING TIME: 1 hour
SERVES 4

METHOD

1 Heat the oil in a saucepan and gently fry the onion until soft. Add the sage, rosemary and bay leaf and fry for a further 1–2 minutes.
2 Stir in the swede, turnip, mooli and carrots and cook for another 5 minutes or until the vegetables are golden.
3 Add the cabbage, stock and stock cube. Cover and cook for 40-50 minutes. Remove the bay leaf, season to taste and serve hot.

FROM TOP: Avocado and lettuce soup; Yogurt and tomato soup; Cucumber and orange soup

14

AVOCADO
◼ AND LETTUCE SOUP ◼

INGREDIENTS

- ◼ ½ pint (300ml) natural yogurt
- ◼ 1 ripe avocado, peeled and stoned
- ◼ juice of one lemon
- ◼ ½ pint (300ml) water
- ◼ salt and pepper
- ◼ 4oz (125g) crisp lettuce
- ◼ 2 tbsp (30ml) chopped chives

Illustrated left

Avocado gives a wonderful flavour and rich creamy texture to cold summer soups, especially when combined with yogurt. The avocado can be watered down considerably to reduce the fat content, without impairing the flavour.

PREPARATION TIME: 20 mins (plus chilling time)

SERVES 4

METHOD

1 In a blender, mix the yogurt, avocado and lemon juice to a smooth paste.
2 Add the water gradually until the mixture has a pouring consistency. Season to taste.
3 Cut the lettuce into fine shreds and mix it into the soup, then add the chives.
4 Serve chilled.

YOGURT
◼ AND TOMATO SOUP ◼

INGREDIENTS

- ◼ 1 red pepper, deseeded
- ◼ 4 tomatoes
- ◼ 4 spring onions
- ◼ ½ pint (300ml) natural yogurt
- ◼ 2 tbsp (30ml) tomato purée
- ◼ dash of Tabasco
- ◼ ¼ pint (150ml) tomato juice (or as required)
- ◼ salt and pepper

GARNISH

- ◼ sesame seeds

Illustrated left

Yogurt is useful for soups and blends well with soft fruit and vegetables. For a good colour, choose red tomatoes and add extra purée, and for a smooth texture, skin the pepper. If you prefer a thinner mixture, add a little more tomato juice.

PREPARATION TIME: 20 mins (plus chilling time)

SERVES 4

METHOD

1 Roast the pepper under a low grill until the skin has charred and will peel off.
2 Scald the tomatoes in boiling water and carefully peel off the loosened skin with a sharp knife. Then chop into small pieces. Trim and chop the spring onions.
3 In a food processor or blender, blend the skinned pepper with all the remaining ingredients until smooth.
4 Season to taste and sprinkle some sesame seeds on top. Serve chilled.

CUCUMBER
◼ AND ORANGE SOUP ◼

INGREDIENTS

- ◼ ⅔ cucumber
- ◼ salt
- ◼ 4 oranges
- ◼ juice of 1–2 lemons
- ◼ ½ pint (300ml) peppermint tea, cold

GARNISH

- ◼ sprig of mint

Illustrated left

A very refreshing, low-fat starter for summer days, this soup is thirst-quenching and easy to digest. The slices of orange and cucumber add to the texture of the soup.

PREPARATION TIME: 30 mins (plus chilling time)

SERVES 4

METHOD

1 Peel the cucumber and slice into slivers. Lay on a flat plate, sprinkle with salt, weigh down with another plate and leave for 20 minutes.
2 Peel 2 oranges and cut into very thin slices.
3 Squeeze the juice from the remaining 2 oranges and mix it with the lemon juice and peppermint tea.
4 Rinse the cucumber. Mix it into the fruited mint mixture, then add the orange slices. Garnish with mint. Serve chilled.

FROM TOP: Raspberry and almond soup; Gazpacho

RASPBERRY AND ALMOND SOUP

INGREDIENTS

- 2 egg yolks
- 1 tbsp (15ml) clear honey
- 1 pint (600ml) skimmed milk
- 4oz (125g) skimmed milk soft cheese (quark)
- 3 drops almond essence
- 8oz (250g) raspberries

GARNISH

- toasted almonds

Illustrated left

This creamy soup makes an unusual starter or dessert. It is sweet and rich-tasting yet contains no sugar, and if you use low-fat milk and low-fat soft cheese, is not too high in fat.

PREPARATION TIME: 30 mins (plus chilling time)

SERVES 4

METHOD

1 Whisk together the egg yolks and honey for about five minutes or until light and frothy.
2 Add the milk very gradually, whisking continuously. Then beat in the cheese and the almond essence to taste.
3 Rinse the raspberries and divide between 4 soup cups, then pour in the almond cream.
4 Serve chilled, garnished with toasted almonds.

GAZPACHO

INGREDIENTS

- ½ small cucumber, peeled and cubed
- 6 tomatoes, skinned and diced
- 6 spring onions, trimmed and chopped
- 1 clove garlic, crushed
- 1 tbsp (15ml) red wine vinegar
- 1 tbsp (15ml) olive oil
- 2 tbsp (30ml) finely chopped fresh parsley
- ¾ pint (450ml) tomato juice
- ¼ tsp ground cinnamon
- 6 cloves
- 1 bay leaf
- ½ tsp soya sauce

Illustrated left

This soup tastes rich, yet is healthily low in fat and high in fibre. For a good strong flavour use tomato juice as a base. To be sure the other flavours develop, leave the soup for a couple of hours before serving.

PREPARATION TIME: 20 mins (plus 2 hours standing time)

SERVES 4

METHOD

1 Prepare the vegetables and mix together in a large bowl.
2 Add the remaining ingredients and mix together gently but thoroughly.
3 Allow the soup to stand for 2 hours, then remove the bay leaf and cloves before serving.

BREAD STICKS (GRISSINI)

INGREDIENTS

- ½oz (15g) fresh yeast
- ¼ pint (150ml) warm water
- 12oz (375g) wholemeal flour
- ½ tsp salt
- 2 tbsp (30ml) olive oil

GLAZE

- a little beaten egg white
- sesame seeds

Illustrated below

Wholemeal Italian bread sticks are an excellent accompaniment to soups, or for buffet-style meals. They also make a healthy alternative to cocktail biscuits or salted nuts.

PREPARATION TIME: 1¼ hours
COOKING TIME: 15 mins
MAKES 15–20 bread sticks

METHOD

1 Whisk the yeast and warm water together. Leave in a warm place for 5–10 minutes to ferment.
2 Sift the flour with the salt into a bowl. Pour over the yeast mixture and oil.
3 Work to a smooth dough and knead well, adding a little more liquid if necessary. Transfer to a clean bowl. Lightly oil the surface of the dough. Cover with clingfilm or a cloth and leave to rise for 20 minutes.
4 Knock back and knead again briefly. Divide the dough into 15–20 pieces. Roll each one out into a very long rope. Place on a greased baking sheet.
5 Cover and leave to prove for 10 minutes. Brush with beaten egg white, then sprinkle with sesame seeds.
6 Bake in a preheated oven at Gas Mark 7, 425°F, 220°C for 15 minutes or until quite crisp. Cool on a wire rack.

Bread sticks (grissini)

■ CRUSTY BREAD ■

INGREDIENTS

■ 2 tsp (10ml) butter
or margarine
■ 4 slices wholemeal
bread

Illustrated right

Warm, crusty bread is a great
accompaniment to almost any hot or cold
soup. This is a quick and easy way to make
the best of stale bread, but the thicker the
bread, the longer it will take to crisp up.

PREPARATION TIME: 5 mins
COOKING TIME: 20 mins
SERVES 4

METHOD

1 Butter the slices of bread and place
them on a baking sheet.
2 Crisp in a preheated oven at Gas Mark
5, 375°F, 190°C for 15–20 minutes.
3 Cool a little and serve while warm.

■ GARLIC BREAD ■

INGREDIENTS

■ 2 cloves garlic,
crushed
■ 4 tsp (20ml) butter
or soft margarine
■ 4 slices of bread or
rounds of French
bread

Illustrated right

Excellent served with garlic-flavoured
soups or with a pâté or spread, garlic
bread is quick and easy to prepare. When
buying garlic, choose plump and juicy
cloves which will yield the best flavour
when cooked.

PREPARATION TIME: 10 mins
COOKING TIME: 15 mins
SERVES 4

METHOD

1 Mix the garlic with the butter or
margarine in a small bowl.
2 Spread the bread on one side with the
garlic butter. Wrap in foil and bake in a
preheated oven at Gas Mark 7, 425°F,
220°C for 15 minutes. Serve hot.

■ CARAWAY SEED ■ ■ TOAST FINGERS ■

INGREDIENTS

■ 4 thin slices of
wholemeal bread
■ 1 tbsp (15ml) butter
or margarine
■ 2 tsp (10ml)
caraway seeds

Illustrated right

These tasty savoury fingers are easy to
make and are best served with a cheesy
soup or one containing caraway seeds. Try
using fennel or aniseeds for variation.

PREPARATION TIME: 5 mins
COOKING TIME: 5 mins
SERVES 4

METHOD

1 Remove the crusts from the slices of
bread.
2 Butter one side and sprinkle with the
caraway seeds.
3 Toast the buttered side under a
preheated grill until golden brown. Cut
into fingers and serve immediately.

■ CHEESE RUSKS ■

INGREDIENTS

■ 4 large thin slices of
wholemeal bread
■ 2–4oz (50–125g)
Cheddar cheese,
finely grated

Illustrated right

With their crunchy texture and savoury
flavour, these rusks make a good
accompaniment to cheesy and vegetable
soups and add extra protein to the first
course.

PREPARATION TIME: 10 mins
COOKING TIME: 20 mins
SERVES 4

METHOD

1 Cover the bread slices with the finely
grated cheese, pressing down with a knife.
2 Place on a baking sheet. Bake in a
preheated oven at Gas Mark 6, 400°F,
200°C for 15–20 minutes until crisp and
golden brown.
3 Cut the crusts off the bread, then cut
neatly into rectangles or triangles.

CLOCKWISE FROM TOP LEFT: Crusty bread; Garlic bread; Herb dumplings; Caraway seed toast fingers; Cheese rusks

■ HERB DUMPLINGS ■

INGREDIENTS

■ 2oz (50g) 85% wholemeal self-raising flour
■ pinch salt
■ ½oz (15g) butter or margarine
■ 1 egg, beaten
■ 1 tbsp (15ml) skimmed milk
■ 1 tbsp (15ml) chopped fresh herbs, such as parsley, dill, rosemary, sage or tarragon
■ black pepper

Illustrated left

Dumplings can be flavoured by an infinite variety of herbs, so select a flavour complementary to the recipe. These dumplings turn a simple soup into a light lunch, or a starter before a light main course. If you do not have wholemeal self-raising flour, use plain wholemeal and add ½ tsp baking powder.

PREPARATION TIME: 15 mins
COOKING TIME: 10 mins
SERVES 4

METHOD

1 Sift the flour with the salt into a bowl. Rub the butter into the flour.
2 Beat the egg with the milk and add the chopped herbs. Mix into the flour mixture and add a little black pepper. Leave to stand for 5 minutes.
3 Drop half-teaspoonfuls of the dough into the simmering soup. Simmer gently for 10 minutes. Turn the dumplings over halfway through the cooking time, so that they cook thoroughly.

CEREALS AND PASTA

A basic dough or batter using wholemeal flour makes pizza-, pasta- and pancake-based meals a good source of fibre, carbohydrate, and protein, and provides a number of important vitamins. There are over 600 types of pasta which are mostly interchangeable, although some, like cannelloni and lasagne, are particularly suited to baking.

TAGLIATELLE VERDE

This is fresh tagliatelle flavoured with spinach for extra taste and colour. Fresh pasta is made with eggs and is soft. Eat soon after purchase.

FUSILLI

Fusilli is pasta made from durum wheat and shaped into spirals (the name means "twists").

TAGLIATELLE

Also known as fettucini, this can be bought fresh or dried.

CANNELLONI

Cannelloni is pasta shaped into hollow tubes which are usually stuffed, baked and served with a sauce.

FUSILLI VERDE

This is made from a dough containing a spinach purée, which boosts the fibre content as well as giving it flavour and colour.

20

MACARONI

This is a term for all dried pasta, but commonly refers to the hollow tubes which can vary greatly in length.

BRAN

Bran is the outer layer of a cereal and is a valuable source of fibre, protein, calcium and iron as well as a number of B Vitamins. It will enrich a wholemeal dough.

WHOLEMEAL FLOUR

This contains protein, fibre and B Vitamins. It makes a delicious nutty pastry and a good base for sauces.

OATMEAL

A good source of protein, fibre, minerals and B Vitamins and delicious in roasts, rissoles, bakes and puddings.

SPAGHETTI

Also known as vermicelli which means "little strings", and available plain, wholemeal and flavoured with spinach.

SEMOLINA

Semolina comes from the starchy part of wheat grain, and is available as medium or coarse meal. Most commonly used for puddings and gnocchi, it also makes a tasty loaf.

PASTA SHELLS

Pasta shells are available plain, wholemeal, flavoured and in varying sizes. They go well with a cheese sauce.

LASAGNE

The name for flat strips of pasta, available plain, wholemeal and flavoured with spinach.

21

BEANS, LENTILS ▪ AND GRAINS ▪

*B*eans, lentils and grains provide the staple food of millions throughout the world. All beans are rich in protein, and when combined with grains, flours, nuts, seeds or dairy produce they provide a very high-quality protein. Most are also rich in fibre, vitamins and minerals. Dried beans should be soaked for 8–12 hours and should be boiled fast for at least 10 minutes before simmering.

BUTTER BEANS

These slightly floury beans are very popular in casseroles, bakes, loaves, salads and purées. A smaller, sweeter relative is the lima bean.

YELLOW SPLIT PEAS

Split peas, like lentils, do not require soaking, and are ideal as a base for soups and casseroles. They contain fibre and Vitamins B_1 and B_2.

CHICK PEAS

Chick peas rival lean meat as a source of protein and contain more calcium than any other bean. A staple food in the Middle East, they have a good balance of amino acids, several minerals and some Vitamin C.

BROWN LENTILS

These lentils are rich in fibre, Vitamin B_6 and folic acid. Unlike green or red split lentils they do not cook to a purée.

GREEN SPLIT PEAS

Split peas are generally sweeter than whole ones, They contain fibre and Vitamins B_1 and B_2 and are delicious in soups, casseroles and bakes.

PORRIDGE OATS

Oat flakes, normally associated with porridge, are made from whole oats which have been steamed, roasted and then rolled. Rich in minerals and B Vitamins.

LONG-GRAIN BROWN RICE

Brown rice is an unrefined carbohydrate, with all the original bran and nutrients. Long-grain rice is used in salads, curries, casseroles and bakes.

RED KIDNEY BEANS

With their floury texture and sweet taste these beans are ideal in spicy loaves, roasts and bakes.

GREEN LENTILS

These large, green lentils are an important part of Indian cooking, as a main or side dish with curry. Like split peas they do not require soaking and contain Vitamin B_6, iron, phosphorus and zinc.

RED SPLIT LENTILS

These small, orange lentils are a staple food throughout the Middle East, often served with rice. They cook to a purée, do not require soaking, and contain Vitamin B_6, iron, fibre, phosphorus and zinc.

POT BARLEY

Pot barley is barley with the outer husks removed, so it retains all the vitamins, minerals and fibre of the grain. The delicious, creamy, nutty taste is ideal for bakes and soups.

HARICOT BEANS

These plump, tender beans contain iron, magnesium and zinc. They can be served in casseroles, purées and salads, and are the original baked bean from Boston.

■ STARTERS ■

CHESTNUT AND ORANGE PATE	26
HOT CUCUMBER WITH PISTACHIO NUTS	26
MAKING GARNISHES	27
FROSTED TOMATO COCKTAIL	27
MELON AND GINGER SORBET	28
NUT PATE	28
CHILLED GRAPEFRUIT WITH MINT	30
SPICED YELLOW PEPPER DIP	30
SAVOURY CHOUX	31
ASPARAGUS SOUFFLE	31
DHAL	33
WALNUT GNOCCHI	33

*FROM TOP: Chestnut and orange pâté (see p.26);
Hot cucumber with pistachio nuts (see p.26)*

CHESTNUT
■ AND ORANGE PATE ■

INGREDIENTS

- ■ 8oz (250g) chestnut purée
- ■ large pinch allspice
- ■ 1 tbsp (15ml) sunflower oil
- ■ 1 onion, peeled and finely chopped
- ■ 2 cloves garlic, crushed
- ■ 4oz (125g) fennel, diced
- ■ 2 tsp (10ml) fresh thyme
- ■ 2oz (50g) wholemeal breadcrumbs
- ■ 2oz (50g) ground almonds
- ■ 2 tsp (10ml) orange rind
- ■ 4 fl oz (125ml) orange juice
- ■ 4 tbsp (60ml) white wine
- ■ 1 egg, beaten
- ■ salt and pepper

Illustrated on page 25

Chestnuts are different from other nuts because they have more starch and much less fat. Their floury taste works well with citrus flavours such as orange juice, and pungent spices such as allspice. You will find the flavour of this pâté develops a day after baking.

PREPARATION TIME: 15 mins
COOKING TIME: 35–45 mins
SERVES 6

METHOD

1 Mix the purée with the allspice to taste.
2 Heat the oil in a pan and gently fry the onion and garlic until soft and translucent. Add the fennel and cook for 3–5 minutes.
3 Mix the cooked onion and fennel with the chestnut purée and blend together.
4 Stir in all the remaining ingredients except the egg, to form a fairly moist mixture. Mix in the egg, then season well.
5 Spoon the mixture into a well-greased 1lb (500g) loaf tin. Bake in a preheated oven at Gas Mark 4, 350°F, 180°C for 35–45 minutes. Leave in the tin to cool, then turn out.

HOT CUCUMBER
■ WITH PISTACHIO NUTS ■

INGREDIENTS

- ■ 1 medium cucumber
- ■ 4oz (125g) pistachio nuts or almonds
- ■ 2 tsp (10ml) olive oil
- ■ 4 medium tomatoes, skinned and chopped
- ■ 4 tbsp (60ml) red wine
- ■ salt and pepper

Illustrated on page 25

The crisp nuts make a good contrast to the cucumber, which is served hot, having been lightly baked.

PREPARATION TIME: 20 mins
COOKING TIME: 15–20 mins
SERVES 4

METHOD

1 Slice the cucumber in half lengthwise, scoop out the centre and cut into thick wedges.
2 Lightly toast the nuts under the grill for 2–3 minutes, then chop. Mix with the olive oil, tomatoes and red wine. Season.
3 Spoon a little filling into each cucumber boat. Place in a lightly greased baking dish and bake in a preheated oven at Gas Mark 6, 400°F, 200°C for 15–20 minutes.

MAKING GARNISHES

*G*arnishes are an important part of any meal, because they can so dramatically enhance the appearance of a dish. The visual appeal is essential if you are trying to change to healthier eating habits for yourself, family or friends. A sprinkling of herbs, grated cheese or chopped nuts will take no time at all, while more complicated garnishes such as carefully prepared vegetables or fruits, roasted seeds, or wholemeal croutôns take a little longer. But any time spent on a garnish is well-rewarded by the differences to the end result.

1 *Use the tip of a sharp knife to split or slice nuts; and a food processor, electric grinder or nut mill to crush them.*

2 *To make croûtons, dice ½ inch (1cm) thick slices of bread into small squares. Fry, grill or dry-bake until gold.*

3 *For raw vegetable garnishes, try pepper rings, cauliflower florets or twists of carrot parings.*

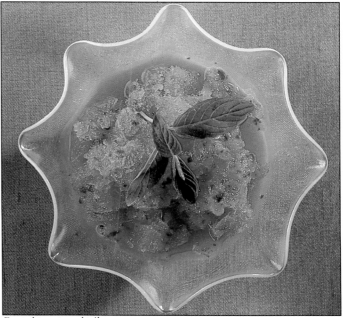

Frosted tomato cocktail

FROSTED TOMATO COCKTAIL

INGREDIENTS

- ¾ pint (450ml) tomato juice
- 1 tbsp (15ml) chopped fresh mint
- 1 tsp (5ml) lemon juice
- 1 tsp (5ml) soya sauce
- salt and black pepper

GARNISH
- few sprigs of mint

Illustrated above

This tomato water ice, flavoured with lemon and mint, makes a refreshing, low-calorie start to a summer meal. It is also quick, easy and cheap to prepare.
PREPARATION TIME: 5 mins (plus 4½ hours' freezing and softening time)
SERVES 4

METHOD

1 Mix together the tomato juice, chopped mint, lemon juice and soya sauce in a bowl or jug. Season to taste. Transfer into a freezerproof container. Cover and freeze for about 4 hours until solid.
2 Remove water ice from the freezer and leave at room temperature for 20–30 minutes to soften slightly. Then crush the ice finely.
3 Pile the crushed tomato ice into individual dishes or glasses. Garnish with sprigs of mint and serve at once.

Melon and ginger sorbet

MELON AND GINGER SORBET

INGREDIENTS

- ½ honeydew melon
- ½ cantaloupe melon
- ½ tsp ground ginger
- ⅛ tsp ground cinnamon
- juice of 1 lime
- 2 egg whites

GARNISH
- lime rind

Illustrated above

This sweet yet sharp sorbet with its light, soft texture helps to stimulate the appetite. Extremely low in calories, it makes a light starter.

PREPARATION TIME: 30 mins (plus about 4 hours' freezing time)
COOKING TIME: 15 mins
SERVES 6–8

METHOD

1 Remove the seeds from the melons and scoop out the flesh. Coarsely chop the flesh and place in a saucepan with the ginger, cinnamon and lime juice. Cover and cook over a low heat for 10–15 minutes or until soft. Cool slightly.
2 Purée the cooked melon in a blender or food processor until smooth and pour into a freezerproof bowl. Freeze for 2 hours.
3 Whisk the egg whites until stiff, whisk the melon purée, then fold the whites into the purée. Transfer to a shallow, freezerproof container. Return the purée to the freezer for at least 2 hours.
4 Serve in individual dishes and garnish with curls of lime rind.

■ NUT PATE ■

INGREDIENTS

- ½oz (15g) butter or margarine
- 1 small onion, peeled and chopped
- 2 large mushrooms, wiped and chopped
- 1 large tomato, skinned and chopped
- ½ tbsp (7.5ml) wholemeal flour
- 3 fl oz (75ml) stock or water
- 1 tsp (5ml) yeast extract
- 1 tsp (5ml) chopped fresh mixed herbs
- 2oz (50g) hazelnuts
- 1oz (25g) unsalted cashew nuts
- 1oz (25g) almonds
- 2oz (50g) wholemeal breadcrumbs
- 1 egg, beaten
- salt and black pepper

GLAZE (optional)
- ½ tsp agar-agar powder (agar-agar is a vegetarian equivalent of gelatine)
- ½ tsp yeast extract

GARNISH
- slices of tomato

Illustrated right

This mixed nut pâté makes a nutritious and filling starter. It is equally good for picnics and packed lunches as it has a firm texture and transports well.

PREPARATION TIME: 30 mins
COOKING TIME: 45–50 mins
SERVES 4

METHOD

1 Melt the butter in a saucepan and gently fry the onion until soft.
2 Add the mushrooms and cook for a further 2–3 minutes. Stir in the tomato, cover and simmer for 5 minutes.
3 Sprinkle the flour over the mixture and cook for 2–3 minutes, stirring. Add the stock, yeast extract and mixed herbs and cook for another 5 minutes.
4 Meanwhile, grind the nuts in a food processor or electric grinder. Add to the vegetable mixture, together with the breadcrumbs. Mix in the egg and season to taste. Leave to stand for 10 minutes.
5 Pack the mixture in a terrine, cover with greased paper and foil and secure them with string. Steam for 45–50 minutes in a big pan. When cool turn out.
6 Dissolve the agar-agar powder in a little water and simmer for 1–2 minutes. Add the yeast extract. Pour over the pâté and leave to cool thoroughly. Serve garnished with slices of tomato.

FROM TOP: Chilled grapefruit with mint (see p.30); Nut pâté

CHILLED GRAPEFRUIT WITH MINT

INGREDIENTS

■ 2 grapefruits
■ 2 pink grapefruits
■ 2 oranges

GLAZE
■ 2 tsp (10ml) arrowroot
■ 2 tsp (10ml) clear honey
■ 2 tsp (10ml) sesame or poppy seeds

GARNISH
■ sprigs of fresh mint

Illustrated on page 29

A honey and sesame seed glaze brings sweetness to the acid fruit.
PREPARATION TIME: 25 mins
COOKING TIME: 5 mins
SERVES 4

METHOD

1 Cut the grapefruits and oranges in half. Cut into segments, between the membranes. Reserve the juice and spoon the segments into 4 grapefruit shells.
2 For the glaze, mix the arrowroot with the reserved fruit juice. Add the honey. Bring the mixture to the boil and simmer for 1–2 minutes. Cool slightly. Pour over the fruit and leave to cool.
3 Meanwhile, toast the seeds under a grill until they start to jump. Sprinkle over the fruit. Garnish and serve chilled.

■ SPICED YELLOW PEPPER DIP ■

INGREDIENTS

■ 1 large yellow pepper, skinned
■ ½ tsp coriander seeds
■ ¼-½ tsp mustard seeds
■ 4 sticks white celery, trimmed and finely chopped
■ 2 fl oz (50ml) natural yogurt
■ 2 tsp (10ml) lemon juice
■ salt and white pepper

GARNISH
■ ring of yellow pepper or fresh coriander leaves

Illustrated right

This low-fat dip has an unusual flavour and is good served with crudités (strips of raw vegetables) before a meal or for a buffet.
PREPARATION TIME: 20 mins
COOKING TIME: 20 mins
SERVES 4

METHOD

1 Put the yellow pepper in a preheated oven at Gas Mark 5, 375°F, 190°C for 20 minutes or until the skin comes off easily.
2 Fry the coriander and mustard seeds gently in an ungreased frying pan until they turn a shade darker.
3 Halve and deseed the pepper, then chop it into small pieces and mix with the celery, yogurt, coriander seeds, mustard seeds and lemon juice, in a blender or food processor until smooth.
4 Taste and adjust the seasoning. Pour the mixture into a small bowl and leave to cool thoroughly. Garnish and serve with a variety of crudités.

FROM TOP: Savoury choux; Asparagus soufflé; Spiced yellow pepper dip

SAVOURY CHOUX

INGREDIENTS

CHOUX PASTRY
- 1oz (25g) soft margarine
- 5 tbsp (75ml) cold water
- 1¼oz (35g) 85% wholemeal flour
- 1 size 4 egg, beaten
- 1oz (25g) Cheddar cheese, grated
- ¼ tsp wholegrain mustard

FILLING
- 14oz (400g) canned artichoke hearts, drained and finely chopped or mashed
- 12 capers, finely chopped
- 4 medium gherkins
- 1 tsp (5ml) lemon juice

DRESSING
- 2 fl oz (5ml) soured cream or smetana
- 1 tsp (5ml) red wine vinegar

Illustrated left

Serve these cheese choux as soon as possible after baking while they are crisp. The piquant filling adds a contrast in texture.

PREPARATION TIME: 35 mins
COOKING TIME: 25 mins
SERVES 4

METHOD

1 Mix the margarine and water and boil. Remove from the heat and beat in the flour. Gradually add the beaten egg, grated cheese and mustard.
2 Pipe the mixture on to a greased baking sheet and bake in a preheated oven at Gas Mark 7, 425°F, 220°C for 15–20 minutes or until the buns are golden and crisp.
3 Pierce a small hole in the bottom of each choux, turn over and bake for a further 2–3 minutes until they are crisp underneath. Cool on a wire rack.
4 For the filling, mix the chopped artichoke hearts with the capers, gherkins and lemon juice. Taste and season if necessary.
5 Make a slit in the buns and fill with some of the mixture. Cool.
6 For the dressing, mix the soured cream or smetana and vinegar together. Pour the dressing over the buns just before serving.

ASPARAGUS SOUFFLE

INGREDIENTS

- 1½ lb (750g) fresh asparagus, trimmed (or 2 × 10oz/300g cans asparagus)
- ¼ pint (150ml) cooking water (or liquid from the cans of asparagus)
- 1½ tsp (7.5ml) agar-agar powder (agar-agar powder is a vegetarian equivalent of gelatine)
- 8 fl oz (250ml) soured cream or smetana
- salt and black pepper
- 2 egg whites

GARNISH
- 4 asparagus tips

Illustrated left

The mild but distinctive flavour of asparagus blends well with a light soufflé mixture to make a luxurious starter.

PREPARATION TIME: 25 mins
COOKING TIME: 30 mins (plus chilling time)
SERVES 4

METHOD

1 Tie the fresh asparagus into bundles and stand them upright in a saucepan of water, or steam them in a steamer, for about 25 minutes or until tender. Reserve the cooking water.
2 When tender, cut off the tips, reserving 4 for garnish, and mash them thoroughly. Reserve the stalks to make a stock, or discard. Mix the asparagus with the cooking water in a saucepan.
3 Sprinkle over the agar-agar powder and bring to the boil, stirring all the time. Simmer for 1–2 minutes. Cool slightly.
4 Mix the ingredients with the soured cream or smetana in a blender or food processor until smooth. Transfer to a bowl and season.
5 Whisk the egg whites until soft peaks form and fold into the mixture. Dip four individual ramekin dishes in cold water, drain briefly and then pour in the mixture. Chill the soufflés until firm. Garnish with the reserved asparagus tips before serving.

FROM TOP: Dhal; Walnut gnocchi

DHAL

INGREDIENTS

- 8oz (250g) red lentils
- ¾ pint (450ml) water
- 1 bay leaf
- 1 onion, peeled and finely chopped
- 1 clove garlic, crushed
- ¼ tsp grated fresh root ginger
- ¼ tsp turmeric
- 1 tbsp (15ml) sunflower oil
- ½ tsp ground cumin
- pinch chilli powder
- 8oz (250g) mixed vegetables, chopped

GARNISH

- fried onion rings
- lemon wedges

Illustrated left

This is a traditional pâté from India and there are many variations which use different spices and vegetables. It is important to cook the lentils thoroughly, so that they are smooth and creamy. This dish benefits from standing for 24 hours and being reheated. Serve with wholemeal Indian bread or brown rice to make a complete meal.

PREPARATION TIME: 20 mins
COOKING TIME: 1 hour
SERVES 4

METHOD

1 Place the lentils in a large saucepan with the water. Bring to the boil. Remove any scum that forms.
2 Add the bay leaf, half the onion, the garlic, ginger and turmeric. Cook slowly for 1 hour until smooth and the grainy texture has disappeared. Check the water content from time to time.
3 Meanwhile, heat the oil in a pan and fry the remaining onion until lightly browned. Add the cumin, chilli powder and mixed vegetables. Season to taste. Cover and sweat until tender.
4 Add the vegetable mixture to the cooked lentils. Leave to stand in a warm place for 10 minutes. Garnish with fried onions and lemon wedges and serve.

WALNUT GNOCCHI

INGREDIENTS

- 2oz (50g) walnuts
- 2oz (50g) wholemeal breadcrumbs
- 8oz (250g) curd cheese
- 2 tbsp (30ml) semolina
- 1 clove garlic, crushed
- 2 tbsp (30ml) chopped fresh basil
- 1 egg, beaten
- black pepper

GARNISH

- grated Parmesan or Cheddar cheese

Illustrated left

There are many versions of these Italian dumplings, known more exotically as gnocchi. This version is made with walnuts and curd cheese. Gnocchi are quick to prepare and make a good starter, especially for a pasta meal. You could also serve them with a sauce and rice or pasta to make a light supper dish.

PREPARATION TIME: 20 mins
COOKING TIME: 20–25 mins
SERVES 4

METHOD

1 Grind the walnuts and breadcrumbs together to form a fine powder using a food processor or nut mill. Mix in all the remaining ingredients and season well.
2 Bring a large pan of salted water to the boil, then reduce the heat so that the water is simmering.
3 Meanwhile, shape the nut mixture into balls and cook four or five at a time in salted, boiling water. Remove with a slotted spoon after 3-4 minutes, when they have risen to the surface. Keep warm until the remaining gnocchi are cooked.
4 Place in a greased baking dish, sprinkle with finely grated Parmesan or Cheddar cheese and grill for 3–4 minutes, or put in a hot oven at Gas Mark 6, 400°F, 200°C for 5–7 minutes. Serve hot.

MAIN COURSES

CHICK PEA MOUSSAKA	36		AUBERGINE AND MUSHROOM RICE	62
HARICOT BEAN AND OLIVE BAKE	36		SPINACH WITH WALNUTS	63
LAYERED HAZELNUT ROAST	37		CHESTNUT AND MUSHROOM BAKE	64
RED KIDNEY BEAN BURGERS	37		PASTA VERDE	64
STUFFED AUBERGINE ROLLS	38		BASIC PASTA DOUGH	64
STUFFED PEPPERS	38		WHOLEWHEAT SPAGHETTI WITH WALNUT AND PARSLEY SAUCE	65
STUFFING AN AUBERGINE	39			
BUTTER BEAN AND CHEESE QUICHE	39		FRESH HERB SPAGHETTI	65
NUTTY ONION FLAN	40		SPINACH AND CHEESE SPAGHETTI	66
SPINACH AND LENTIL PIE	41		USING A PASTA MACHINE	66
DUTCH BEAN STAMPPOT	43		SPAGHETTI WITH RED LENTIL SAUCE	67
CREAMY HARICOT HOT-POT	43		WHOLEMEAL SPAGHETTI BAKE	67
SWEET AND SOUR BEANS	44		RED LENTIL LASAGNE	68
CHILLI CASSEROLE	44		WHOLEMEAL MACARONI CHEESE WITH FENNEL	69
RATATOUILLE	44		SPICY PEPPER MACARONI	69
SPICY COURGETTES AND PEPPERS	45		MACARONI IN GINGER AND TOMATO SAUCE	70
COURGETTE AND LENTIL GRATIN	46		MAKING TAGLIATELLE	70
CRUMBLETOP	47		VEGETABLE TAGLIATELLE WITH CHEESE AND TOMATO SAUCE	71
RED AND ORANGE CASSEROLE	48		LASAGNE WITH BEAN AND TOMATO SAUCE	71
GIANT WHOLEMEAL SAMOSA	48		AUBERGINE, PEPPER AND MUSHROOM LASAGNE	72
RED BEANS AND OLIVES	50		MAKING RAVIOLI	72
BUTTER BEANS AU GRATIN	50		OLIVE AND TOMATO RAVIOLI	73
HARICOT BEANS WITH APPLE AND CIDER	50		RICE AND EGG CANNELLONI	73
QUICK RED LENTILS	51		SPINACH AND COTTAGE CHEESE RAVIOLI	74
HARICOT BEANS AND TOMATO SAUCE	52		MAKING CANNELLONI	74
CURRIED CHICK PEAS	52		BASIC PIZZA DOUGH	75
CRUNCHY CASSEROLE WITH CHICK PEAS	53		NEAPOLITAN PIZZA	75
AUBERGINE AND BUTTER BEAN BIRYANI	53		PIZZA WITH SPINACH PUREE	75
VEGETABLE AND LENTIL COTTAGE PIE	54		MAKING PIZZA BASES	76
SAVOURY CRUMBLE	55		PIZZA WITH ONION TOPPING	76
BAKED TOMATOES	55		HARICOT BEAN AND PEPPER PIZZA	77
CHINESE BAKE WITH WATERCRESS SAUCE	55		TOMATO AND CHILLI PIZZA	77
BAKED SPANISH OMELETTE	56		MOZZARELLA AND TOMATO PIZZA	77
STUFFED AUBERGINES WITH APRICOTS	56		CHEESE AND LEEK PIZZA	78
CHEESY LEEK AND POTATO CASSEROLE	57		PIZZA POCKETS WITH BROAD BEANS	78
MIXED VEGETABLE CURRY	57		ROLLED PIZZA WITH A NUTTY TOMATO FILLING	79
CHEESE AND WALNUT LOAF	58		PASTRY-BASE PIZZA WITH ROSEMARY SAUCE	79
CAULIFLOWER AND ALMOND BAKE	58		WHOLEMEAL PANCAKE BATTER	80
HAZELNUT LOAF WITH MUSHROOM AND PEPPER SAUCE	59		MAKING PANCAKES	80
COLOURFUL BEAN LOAF WITH CARROT SAUCE	59		AUBERGINE PANCAKES	81
ALMOND WHEEL	60		ARTICHOKE AND HAZELNUT PANCAKES	81
USING A RING MOULD	61		SPICED PANCAKES	81
SHARP RICE WITH MILD SAUCE	61		WHOLEMEAL PANCAKES WITH A SPICY BEAN FILLING	82
ALMOND AND VEGETABLE PAELLA	62		SPLIT PEA AND POTATO PANCAKES	83

FROM TOP: *Chick pea moussaka (see p.36); Haricot bean and olive bake (see p.36)*

CHICK PEA MOUSSAKA

INGREDIENTS

- 4oz (125g) chick peas, soaked, or an 8oz (250g) can
- 12oz (375g) aubergines
- 12oz (375g) potatoes, scrubbed
- 1 tbsp (15ml) olive oil
- 1 onion, peeled and finely chopped
- 2 cloves garlic, crushed
- 14oz (400g) can tomatoes, puréed
- 2 tsp (10ml) dried oregano
- 1 tsp (5ml) finely chopped fresh mint
- 1–2 tbsp (15–30ml) tomato purée
- soya sauce to taste

TOPPING

- 1 tsp (5ml) cumin seeds
- ¼ pint (150ml) natural yogurt
- 1 egg, beaten

Illustrated on page 35

If you are in a hurry use canned chick peas in this popular dish.

PREPARATION TIME: 40 mins (plus 10–12 hours soaking time)

COOKING TIME: 25–30 mins (plus 45–55 mins for the peas)

SERVES 4

METHOD

1 Drain the chick peas and bring to the boil in fresh water. Boil fast for 10 minutes, cover and simmer for 35–45 minutes.

2 Prick and trim the aubergines. Bake in a preheated oven at Gas Mark 4, 350°F, 180°C for 20 minutes, then slice. Boil the potatoes until tender, then slice thickly.

3 Gently fry the onion for 5–7 minutes. Add the garlic and cook for 1 minute. Add the tomatoes, oregano, mint, tomato purée and chick peas. Cook gently for 10 minutes, then season well with soya sauce.

4 Grease a deep 2-pint (1 litre) ovenproof dish and fill with layers of aubergine, potato and chick pea sauce.

5 For the topping, toast the cumin seeds, mix into the yogurt and add the egg. Spoon over the moussaka. Bake in a preheated oven at Gas Mark 4, 350°F, 180°C for 25–30 minutes. Serve hot.

HARICOT BEAN AND OLIVE BAKE

INGREDIENTS

- 6oz (175g) haricot beans, soaked
- 2 tsp (10ml) olive oil
- 1 onion, peeled and finely chopped
- 2 tsp (10ml) garam masala
- 1 tsp (5ml) ground cumin
- ½ tsp chilli powder
- 14oz (400g) can tomatoes, puréed
- 4oz (125g) porridge oats
- 4oz (125g) black olives, chopped
- 3oz (75g) Cheddar cheese, grated
- salt and black pepper

GARNISH

- whole black olives
- finely chopped fresh parsley

Illustrated on page 35

Cumin and other curry flavours, tomatoes and olives all blend particularly well with haricot beans.

PREPARATION TIME: 15 mins (plus 10–12 hours soaking time)

COOKING TIME: 30–40 mins (plus 35–45 mins for the beans)

SERVES 4–6

METHOD

1 Drain the beans and bring to the boil in plenty of fresh water. Boil fast for 10 minutes, cover and simmer for 25–35 minutes. Drain and mash.

2 Heat the oil in a pan and gently fry the onion until just soft. Add the spices and fry for 30 seconds. Add the beans and tomatoes and cook for 5 minutes, then remove from the heat and stir in the oats, olives and 2oz (50g) of the cheese.

3 Season well. Spoon the mixture into a lightly greased, shallow baking dish, cover with the remaining cheese and bake in a preheated oven at Gas Mark 4, 350°F, 180°C for 20–25 minutes. Garnish with black olives and parsley. Serve hot.

Layered hazelnut roast

Red kidney bean burgers

LAYERED HAZELNUT ROAST

INGREDIENTS

- ½oz (15g) sunflower margarine
- ½oz (15g) wholemeal flour
- ¼ pint (150ml) skimmed milk
- 3oz (75g) breadcrumbs
- 2oz (50g) Cheddar cheese, grated
- 1 egg, beaten
- 2 tbsp (30ml) finely chopped fresh parsley
- 1–2 tsp (5–10ml) lemon juice
- pinch chilli powder
- black pepper

FILLING

- 2oz (50g) hazelnuts, coarsely chopped
- 4oz (125g) carrots, scrubbed and diced
- 1 green pepper, deseeded and diced
- 2 tsp (10ml) oil

Illustrated above

The stir-fried vegetables in the filling and the cheese in the loaf itself give this dish a deliciously moist consistency.

PREPARATION TIME: 40 mins
COOKING TIME: 30–40 mins
SERVES 4

METHOD

1 Melt the margarine over a gentle heat, then sprinkle the flour on top. Cook for 2–3 minutes. Add the milk and bring to boiling point, stirring constantly. Reduce the heat and simmer for 2–3 minutes. Allow to cool slightly.
2 Remove from the heat and stir in the breadcrumbs, cheese, beaten egg and herbs. Season the mixture well with lemon juice, chilli powder and black pepper.
3 Quickly stir-fry the prepared nuts and vegetables in the oil until just soft.
4 Lightly grease a 1lb (500g) loaf tin. Spoon in half of the cheese mixture. Cover with the nuts and vegetables, pressing down well. Cover with the remaining cheese mixture.
5 Bake in a preheated oven at Gas Mark 6, 400°F, 200°C for 30–40 minutes or until firm. Cool slightly, then turn out to serve.

RED KIDNEY BEAN BURGERS

INGREDIENTS

- 6oz (175g) red kidney beans, soaked
- 4oz (125g) brown rice
- 1 small onion, diced
- 1 clove garlic, crushed
- 2 tsp (10ml) soya sauce
- 1 tsp (5ml) olive oil
- 1 tsp (5ml) wholegrain mustard
- ½ tsp grated fresh root ginger
- juice of ½ lemon
- 3 tbsp (45ml) tomato purée
- salt and black pepper

Illustrated above

These high-fibre burgers are delicious with potatoes and vegetables.

PREPARATION TIME: 1 hour (plus 10–12 hours soaking time)
COOKING TIME: 10–20 mins (plus 40–50 mins for the beans)
MAKES 8–10 burgers

METHOD

1 Drain the beans, boil fast for 10 minutes, cover and simmer for 30–40 minutes. Drain well. Meanwhile, cook the rice in twice its volume of boiling water, covered, for 25 minutes.
2 Blend the beans, onion, garlic, soya sauce, oil, mustard, ginger, lemon juice and tomato purée. Stir in the rice and season well. Chill the mixture for ½ an hour so that it firms up a little.
3 Shape into 8–10 burgers and bake for 20 minutes in a preheated oven at Gas Mark 4, 350°F, 180°C. Turn after 10 minutes. Alternatively, fry in a very small amount of oil for 10 minutes.

FROM TOP: *Stuffed aubergine rolls; Stuffed peppers*

STUFFED AUBERGINE ROLLS

INGREDIENTS

- 1½lb (750g) large aubergines
- 6oz (175g) button mushrooms, diced
- 6oz (175g) bean sprouts
- 1 large red pepper, finely diced
- 1 clove garlic, crushed
- 2 tsp (10ml) soya sauce
- 1 tsp (5ml) grated root ginger
- 1 tbsp (15ml) olive oil
- 1 onion, finely chopped
- 1lb (500g) tomatoes, chopped
- 1–2 tbsp (15–30ml) tomato purée
- 1 bay leaf
- 1 tsp (5ml) oregano
- salt and black pepper

Illustrated left

Aubergines and tomatoes complement each other in flavour, in colour and in texture.

PREPARATION TIME: 50 mins
COOKING TIME: 20 mins
SERVES 4

METHOD

1 Thinly slice the aubergines lengthways, sprinkle with salt and leave face down for 15–20 minutes. Rinse, then blanch them.
2 For the filling, mix the mushrooms, bean sprouts, red pepper, garlic, soya sauce and ginger together in a bowl.
3 For the sauce, gently fry the onion for 4–5 minutes. Add the tomatoes, purée and herbs and simmer for 30 minutes. Season well.
4 Put 1 tbsp (15ml) of filling on each aubergine slice and roll up. Place in a greased ovenproof dish with the seam facing downwards. Pour on the sauce, cover and bake in a preheated oven at Gas Mark 6, 400°F, 200°C for 20 minutes. Serve hot.

STUFFED PEPPERS

INGREDIENTS

- 4 red or green peppers
- ½oz (15g) margarine
- ½oz (15g) wholemeal flour
- ¼ pint (150ml) skimmed milk
- 4oz (125g) hazelnuts, chopped
- 2 small dessert apples, diced
- 4 large sticks celery, trimmed and diced
- 4 spring onions, trimmed and chopped
- 2–3 tsp (10–15ml) fresh dill weed
- salt and pepper

Illustrated left

In this dish, peppers are filled with hazelnuts, apple and celery.

PREPARATION TIME: 20 mins
COOKING TIME: 25–30 mins
SERVES 4

METHOD

1 Slice the lids off the tops of the peppers, then plunge them into boiling water for 5 minutes. Drain.
2 Melt the margarine and sprinkle on the flour. Cook for 2–3 minutes. Stir in the milk and simmer for 3–4 minutes. Remove from the heat, mix in the remaining ingredients and season.
2 Divide the filling between the four peppers. Place in a deep ovenproof dish with a little water. Cover with foil and bake in a preheated oven at Gas Mark 5, 375°F, 190°C for 25–30 minutes. Serve hot.

STUFFING
AN AUBERGINE

*S*cooped-out vegetables and fruits make a convenient and attractive way of serving a dish. Aubergine plays an essential part in Mediterranean food, although it actually originates from Asia. Stuffed aubergine is a traditional dish in Greece and Turkey, where it is often served with minced meat; apricots and lentils are another authentic filling. The beautiful colour of the skin makes this dish look most appetizing.

1 *Slash the aubergine flesh, taking care not to damage the skin. Scoop out and chop finely.*

2 *Heat the oil and spices in a pan. Add the other ingredients and cook as directed in the recipe.*

3 *Spoon the mixture back into the aubergine halves. Cover and bake.*

BUTTER BEAN
AND CHEESE QUICHE

INGREDIENTS

■ 4oz (125g) butter beans, soaked

PASTRY
■ 4oz (125g) wholemeal flour
■ pinch salt
■ 2oz (50g) margarine
■ 2–3 tbsp (30–45ml) cold water
■ 1 tsp (5ml) sunflower oil
■ 1 tsp (5ml) lemon juice

FILLING
■ 4 sticks celery, trimmed and chopped
■ 2 eggs, beaten
■ 2 fl oz (50ml) skimmed milk
■ 2oz (50g) Cheddar cheese, grated
■ ¼ tsp (10ml) nutmeg
■ 2 tsp (10ml) white wine vinegar
■ 1 tsp (5ml) wholemeal flour
■ salt and black pepper

Illustrated on page 40

This highly nutritious, creamy flan makes an excellent lunch or supper dish, accompanied by a salad. The beans and celery both add fibre and flavour to the filling.

PREPARATION TIME: 35 mins (plus 10–12 hours soaking time)
COOKING TIME: 25–30 mins (plus 40–50 mins for the beans)
SERVES 4

METHOD

1 Drain the beans. Place in a pan with plenty of fresh water. Bring to the boil and boil fast for 10 minutes, then cover and simmer for 30–40 minutes. Drain well.
2 For the pastry, mix the flour and salt together in a large bowl. Rub in the margarine until the mixture resembles fine breadcrumbs. Mix together the water, oil and lemon juice. Sprinkle on to the flour mixture. Quickly draw together to make a soft dough. Wrap in clingfilm and chill for 20 minutes.
3 For the filling, mix all the filling ingredients with the butter beans and season to taste.
4 Roll out the dough and use to line an 8-inch (20cm) flan ring. Prick well and bake in a preheated oven at Gas Mark 6, 400°F, 200°C for 4 minutes.
5 Spoon in the filling and bake for another 25–30 minutes. Leave to set for 5 minutes before serving.

FROM TOP: Nutty onion flan; Butter bean and cheese quiche (see p.39)

NUTTY ONION FLAN

INGREDIENTS

BASE
- 4oz (125g) almonds
- 4oz (125g) low-fat Cheddar-type cheese
- 6oz (175g) wholemeal breadcrumbs
- pinch chilli powder
- 1–2 tbsp (15–30ml) sunflower oil

FILLING
- 1 tbsp (15ml) sunflower oil
- 1lb (500g) onions, finely chopped
- 1 tsp (5ml) wholemeal flour
- 1 tsp (5ml) French mustard
- 2 tsp (10ml) lemon juice
- 2 eggs, beaten
- ½ pint (300ml) natural yogurt
- 3 tbsp (45ml) finely chopped fresh parsley
- salt and black pepper

Illustrated left

The cheese, nuts and spice in the base add protein and flavour to this savoury flan and complement the sharp flavour of the onion, mustard and yogurt in the filling.

PREPARATION TIME: 30 mins
COOKING TIME: 20 mins
SERVES 8

METHOD

1 Grind together the almonds, cheese and breadcrumbs in a coffee grinder or food processor. Mix in the chilli powder and oil to form a light crumble.
2 Press the mixture into a 10–inch (25cm) flan ring and bake in a preheated oven for 10 minutes at Gas Mark 6, 400°F, 200°C.
3 For the filling, heat the oil in a pan and fry the onion for 10 minutes. Add the flour and cook for 2–3 minutes. Remove from the heat.
4 Stir in the mustard and lemon juice. Beat the egg and yogurt together. Mix with the onion mixture and stir in the parsley. Season to taste.
5 Spoon into the flan and bake in a preheated oven for 20 minutes at Gas Mark 6, 400°F, 200°C. Serve hot or cold.

SPINACH AND LENTIL PIE

INGREDIENTS

- 6oz (175g) red lentils
- ¾ pint (450ml) water
- 1½lb (750g) fresh spinach, washed and shredded
- 6oz (175g) curd cheese

SAUCE
- 1oz (25g) margarine
- ½oz (15g) wholemeal flour
- ½ pint (300ml) skimmed milk
- sprig of thyme
- bay leaf
- ¼ tsp grated nutmeg
- salt and black pepper

PASTRY
- 4oz (125g) wholemeal flour
- pinch salt
- 2oz (50g) margarine
- 2–3 tbsp (30–45ml) cold water
- 1 tsp (5ml) sunflower oil
- 1 tsp (5ml) lemon juice

Illustrated right

A nutritious pie combining wholemeal pastry with a colourful spinach filling and a creamy cheese sauce. Serve this hot as a supper dish with potatoes and side vegetables.

PREPARATION TIME: 45 mins
COOKING TIME: 25–30 mins (plus 15 mins for the lentils)
SERVES 4

METHOD

1 Place the lentils in the water and bring to the boil. Remove any scum if necessary. Cook for 15 minutes or until the lentils form a soft purée. Beat well with a wooden spoon.

2 Lightly cook the washed spinach without extra water in a large, covered pan for 3–4 minutes or until just wilted.

3 Mix together the cooked lentils, spinach and curd cheese.

4 For the sauce, melt the margarine in a pan and add the flour. Stir and cook for 3–4 minutes.

5 Gradually pour on the skimmed milk, stirring constantly, and bring the sauce to boiling point.

6 Add the herbs and nutmeg, then simmer for 3–4 minutes. Season well.

7 Mix the sauce with the lentil and spinach mixture. Spoon the filling into a lightly greased ovenproof dish.

8 For the pastry, mix the flour and salt together in a large bowl. Rub in the margarine until the mixture resembles fine breadcrumbs. Mix together the water, oil and lemon juice. Sprinkle on to the flour mixture. Quickly draw together to make a soft dough. Wrap in clingfilm and chill for 20 minutes.

9 Roll out the pastry and use for the top. Prick well and brush with some beaten egg. Bake in a preheated oven at Gas Mark 6, 400°F, 200°C for 25–30 minutes.

Spinach and lentil pie

FROM TOP: *Dutch bean stamppot; Creamy haricot hot-pot*

DUTCH BEAN STAMPPOT

INGREDIENTS

- 6oz (175g) red kidney beans, soaked
- 1 tbsp (15ml) sunflower oil
- 1 onion, peeled and finely chopped
- 4 sticks celery, trimmed and diced
- 8oz (250g) carrots, scrubbed and diced
- 14oz (400g) can tomatoes, puréed
- 1 bay leaf
- 1 tsp (5ml) dried thyme
- 2 tbsp (30ml) finely chopped fresh parsley
- salt and pepper
- 1 tsp (5ml) yeast extract
- 12oz (375g) potatoes, mashed

Illustrated left

A stamppot is a traditional Dutch recipe with a rich bean base.

PREPARATION TIME: 30 mins (plus 10-12 hours soaking time)

COOKING TIME: 15–20 mins (plus 50 mins for the beans)

SERVES 4

METHOD

1 Drain the beans. Boil fast in fresh water for 10 minutes. Cover and simmer for 30–40 minutes. Drain and reserve the stock.

2 Heat the oil and gently fry the onion for 3–4 minutes or until soft. Add the celery, carrots and cooked beans and cook for 5 minutes. Stir in the tomatoes, bay leaf, thyme and parsley.

3 Dissolve the yeast extract in a little hot bean stock and stir in. Bring to the boil and simmer for 20 minutes. Season to taste.

4 Place the stamppot in a lightly greased ovenproof dish, cover with the mashed potato and bake in a preheated oven at Gas Mark 4, 350°F, 180°C for 15–20 minutes.

CREAMY HARICOT HOT-POT

INGREDIENTS

- 6oz (175g) haricot beans, soaked
- 1 tbsp (15ml) sunflower oil
- 8oz (250g) leeks, trimmed and chopped
- 4 sticks celery, trimmed and diced
- 8oz (250g) carrots, chopped
- 8oz (250g) sweetcorn kernels, fresh, canned or frozen
- 2 medium potatoes, scrubbed and diced
- 2 tsp (10ml) fresh dill
- 1 tbsp (15ml) fresh thyme
- 3 tbsp (45ml) chopped fresh parsley
- ½ pint (300ml) bean stock
- ½ pint (300ml) skimmed milk
- salt and pepper

Illustrated left

A colourful casserole that combines beans and sweetcorn to make a rich source of protein. Serve with lightly steamed broccoli or other vegetables.

PREPARATION TIME: 10 mins (plus 10–12 hours soaking time)

COOKING TIME: 30–40 mins (plus 40–50 mins for the beans)

SERVES 4

METHOD

1 Drain the beans. Bring to the boil in fresh water and boil fast for 10 minutes, then cover and simmer for a further 30–40 minutes. Drain and reserve the stock.

2 Heat the oil and gently fry the leeks for 3–4 minutes. Add the celery, carrots, sweetcorn kernels and cooked beans. Cook for 3–4 minutes.

3 Add the potatoes, herbs, stock and milk. Bring to boiling point, then simmer uncovered, for 30–40 minutes, or until all the vegetables are tender. Season and serve hot.

Sweet and sour beans

SWEET AND SOUR BEANS

INGREDIENTS
- 6oz (175g) haricot beans, soaked
- 1 tbsp (15ml) sunflower oil
- 8oz (250g) leeks, cleaned and diced
- 8oz (250g) carrots, chopped
- 8oz (250g) turnips, chopped
- 1 red pepper, deseeded and sliced
- 3 tbsp (45ml) arrowroot or cornflour
- 3 tbsp (45ml) sherry
- 3 tbsp (45ml) soya sauce
- 7 fl oz (200ml) bean stock
- 8 fl oz (250ml) apple juice
- 4 fl oz (125ml) wine vinegar
- juice of 1 orange
- 1 tsp (5ml) ground cardamom
- ½ inch (1cm) fresh root ginger, grated
- 2 cloves garlic, crushed

Illustrated above

Beans are an excellent source of protein and go well with this sweet and sour sauce.
PREPARATION TIME: 15 mins (plus 10–12 hours soaking time)
COOKING TIME: 15 mins (plus 40–50 mins for the beans)
SERVES 4

METHOD
1 Drain the beans. Place in a pan with plenty of fresh water. Bring to the boil and boil fast for 10 minutes, then cover and simmer for 30–40 minutes. Add more water if necessary. Drain, reserving the stock.
2 Heat the oil and gently fry the leeks, carrots, turnips, pepper and cooked beans for 10 minutes.
3 Mix all the remaining ingredients together, making sure all the arrowroot or cornflour is completely dissolved.
4 Add the sauce and bring to the boil, stirring constantly. Cook until the sauce has thickened and cleared. Season to taste and serve hot.

CHILLI CASSEROLE

INGREDIENTS
- 6oz (175g) red kidney beans, soaked
- 1 tbsp (15ml) olive oil
- 2 onions, peeled and finely chopped
- 2 cloves garlic, crushed
- 1 green chilli, deseeded and diced
- 1 tsp (5ml) mustard powder
- 1 tsp (5ml) cumin seeds
- 1 cinnamon stick
- ½ tsp celery seeds or 2 sticks celery, finely chopped
- 8oz (250g) red cabbage, finely shredded
- 14oz (400g) can chopped tomatoes
- salt and pepper

Illustrated right

This casserole is rich in colour and flavour and easy to prepare. Serve with brown rice, noodles or corn bread for a good supper dish.
PREPARATION TIME: 10 mins (plus 10–12 hours soaking time)
COOKING TIME: 30–40 mins (plus 40–50 mins for the beans)
SERVES 4

METHOD
1 Drain the kidney beans. Place in a pan with plenty of fresh water. Bring to the boil and boil fast for 10 minutes. Cover and simmer for 30-40 minutes or until soft. Drain well.
2 Gently fry the onion for 3–4 minutes or until soft. Add the garlic, chilli and spices and fry for 2 minutes.
3 Stir in the cabbage, kidney beans and tomatoes. Heat through and cook for 30–40 minutes until the cabbage is tender. Remove the cinnamon stick, season and serve hot.

RATATOUILLE

INGREDIENTS
- 1 tbsp (15ml) olive oil
- 1 onion, chopped
- 2 cloves garlic, crushed
- 1 medium aubergine, diced
- 4 courgettes, sliced
- 2 red peppers, deseeded and diced
- 14oz (400g) can tomatoes
- 1 bay leaf
- sprig of fresh thyme
- 2–3oz (50–75g) pine kernels or sunflower seeds
- salt and pepper

Illustrated right

A very popular dish in Mediterranean cuisine. Serve with brown rice.
PREPARATION TIME: 50 mins
COOKING TIME: 40 mins
SERVES 4

METHOD
1 Heat the oil in a pan and gently fry the onion for a few minutes.
2 Add the garlic, aubergine, courgettes and peppers. Cook for 10 minutes, stirring occasionally.
3 Add the tomatoes and herbs and cook gently for 40 minutes until the vegetables are fairly soft.
4 Stir in the pine kernels or sunflower seeds, season well and serve immediately.

SPICY COURGETTES AND PEPPERS

INGREDIENTS

- 2oz (50g) creamed coconut
- 1 tbsp (15ml) sunflower oil
- 2 onions, peeled and finely chopped
- 3 cloves garlic, crushed
- 1 inch (2.5cm) fresh root ginger, grated
- 1 tsp (5ml) ground coriander
- 1 tsp (5ml) garam masala
- 1 tsp (5ml) turmeric
- 1 red pepper, deseeded and diced
- 1 green pepper deseeded and diced
- 1lb (500g) courgettes, diced
- 8 tomatoes, skinned and chopped
- juice of ½ a lemon
- 4oz (125g) sultanas
- 2oz (50g) cashew nuts
- salt and pepper

Illustrated left

Serve with brown rice or wholemeal Indian breads to make a complete meal.
PREPARATION TIME: 20 mins
COOKING TIME: 30–40 mins
SERVES 4

METHOD

1 Grate the coconut, dissolve in ½ a pint (300ml) of boiling water.
2 Heat the oil and gently fry the onions for 4–5 minutes or until quite soft. Add the garlic and root ginger. Mix the spices with a little water to form a paste and add to the onions. Cook for 3 minutes.
3 Add the peppers, courgettes and tomatoes to the pan. Cover and sweat for 10 minutes.
4 Stir in the coconut milk, lemon juice, sultanas and nuts. Simmer uncovered for 30–40 minutes. Season.

FROM TOP: Chilli casserole; Spicy courgettes and peppers; Ratatouille

COURGETTE
■ AND LENTIL GRATIN ■

INGREDIENTS

- 4oz (125g) red lentils
- 1 tbsp (15ml) olive oil
- 1 onion, peeled and finely chopped
- 1 clove garlic, crushed
- 1 tbsp (15ml) tomato purée
- 2oz (50g) porridge oats
- 1 tbsp (15ml) lemon juice
- 2 tsp (10ml) chopped mixed herbs (eg, sage, thyme, majoram)

FILLING

- 8oz (250g) courgettes, diced
- 2 eggs, beaten
- 1 tbsp (15ml) wholemeal flour
- 2 fl oz (50ml) skimmed milk
- salt and pepper
- 2oz (50g) Cheddar cheese, grated

Illustrated right

Cooked lentils are quite floury in texture and when mixed with oats and tomato purée, make a mixture that is thick enough to be used as an alternative to pastry. Lentils combine especially well with a creamy vegetable sauce, such as the egg and courgette filling used here.

PREPARATION TIME: 40 mins
COOKING TIME: 20–25 mins
SERVES 4

METHOD

1 Cook the lentils in twice their volume of water for about 10 minutes, or until they are fairly soft. Beat well with a wooden spoon, then drain.
2 Heat the oil in a pan and gently fry the onion for 3–4 minutes or until soft. Add the garlic and fry for 2 minutes.
3 Remove from the heat and mix in the cooked lentils, tomato purée, oats, lemon juice and herbs. Season well. The mixture should be thick enough to hold together. If the lentils are a little wet, return the pan to the heat to dry out, or add a few more oat flakes.
4 Press the mixture around the sides and base of an 8-inch (20cm) flan dish.
5 For the filling, lightly steam the courgettes for 4 minutes or until tender.
6 Blend the eggs with the flour, then add the milk. Stir in the cooked courgettes and season well.
7 Spoon the filling into the flan case. Cover with grated cheese.
8 Bake in a preheated oven at Gas Mark 5, 375°F, 190°C for 20–25 minutes or until the filling has set. Serve hot.

FROM LEFT: Courgette and lentil gratin; Crumbletop

CRUMBLETOP

INGREDIENTS

- 1oz (25g) margarine
- ½oz (15g) wholemeal flour
- ½ pint (300ml) skimmed milk
- ¼ tsp nutmeg
- pinch mustard powder
- 1lb (500g) cauliflower, broken into florets
- 8oz (250g) sweetcorn kernels, fresh, canned or frozen
- 8oz (250g) Jerusalem artichokes, peeled and diced
- 1–2oz (25–50g) nuts (pine kernels, cashews or almonds)
- salt and pepper

TOPPING

- 2oz (50g) wholemeal flour
- 2oz (50g) porridge oats
- 2oz (50g) ground nuts
- 3 tbsp (45–50ml) sunflower oil

Illustrated left

A good way to use nuts in savoury vegetable dishes is to keep some of them whole and grind the rest and add them to crumble-type toppings. This enriches the mixture and increases the protein content. This topping could be used on a wide range of dishes, and could also be used as a nutty base instead of pastry. Nuts are an excellent source of protein and provide a number of valuable vitamins and minerals. In a crunchy recipe like this, it is a good idea to undercook the vegetables so that the base has plenty of texture and fewer nutrients are lost during cooking.

PREPARATION TIME: 40 mins
COOKING TIME: 15 mins
SERVES 4

METHOD

1 Melt the margarine in a pan and sprinkle on the flour. Cook for 3–4 minutes.

2 Gradually add the milk and bring the sauce to boiling point, stirring constantly. Simmer for 3–4 minutes, stirring. Season with nutmeg and mustard.

3 Lightly steam the cauliflower, sweetcorn and artichokes for 8–10 minutes until tender.

4 Mix them, together with the nuts, into the sauce and season well.

5 For the topping, mix the dry ingredients together, then work in the oil with your fingertips to form a light crumble.

6 Spoon the vegetables into a lightly greased 2 pint (1 litre) ovenproof dish and cover with crumble topping.

7 Bake in a preheated oven at Gas Mark 6, 400°F, 200°C for 15 minutes or until the topping is well browned.

Red and orange casserole

RED AND ❚ ORANGE CASSEROLE ❚

INGREDIENTS

■ 8oz (250g) red
kidney beans, soaked
■ 2 tsp (10ml)
sunflower oil
■ 1 onion, chopped
■ 1 yellow pepper,
deseeded and cut
into strips
■ 3 medium carrots,
sliced
■ 2 tsp (10ml)
ground cinnamon
■ 14oz (400g) can of
chopped tomatoes
■ ¼pt (150ml) red
kidney bean stock
■ 2 tsp (10ml)
chopped fresh thyme
■ 1 tsp (5ml) soya
sauce
■ grated rind and
juice of 2 oranges
■ salt and pepper

Illustrated above

This colourful high-fibre recipe is made
up of an unusual combination of beans
and vegetables, flavoured with oranges. If
yellow peppers are not available, use red
or green. Serve with noodles and steamed
vegetables.
PREPARATION TIME: 15 mins (plus 10–12
hours soaking time)
COOKING TIME: 20 mins (plus 45 mins for
the beans)
SERVES 4

METHOD

1 Drain the beans. Put into a saucepan
with fresh water. Bring to the boil and boil
fast for 10 minutes. Reduce the heat, cover
and simmer for 35 minutes. Drain,
reserving the stock.
2 Heat the oil in a large pan and fry the
onion for 5 minutes. Add the pepper,
carrots and cooked beans and cook for 3–4
minutes.
3 Add the cinnamon, then the tomatoes,
bean stock, thyme and soya sauce. Cover
and simmer for 20 minutes.
4 Add the orange rind and juice. Season
and serve hot.

❚ GIANT WHOLEMEAL SAMOSA ❚

INGREDIENTS
FILLING
■ 6oz (175g) lentils,
soaked
■ 2 medium potatoes,
diced
■ 2 tsp (10ml)
sunflower oil
■ 1 large onion,
chopped
■ 1 tsp (5ml) cumin
seeds
■ 2 cloves garlic,
chopped
■ 1 tbsp (15ml) mild
curry powder
■ ¼ pint (150ml)
vegetable stock or
water
■ 1 tbsp (15ml) soya
sauce
PASTRY
■ 8oz (250g)
wholemeal flour
■ 2oz (50g) butter or
margarine
■ 2oz (50g) white
vegetable fat
■ pinch chilli powder
■ 5–6 tbsp (75–90ml)
cold water

Illustrated right

Light wholemeal pastry is here filled with a
spicy mixture of lentils and potatoes and
garnished with parsley.
PREPARATION TIME: 45 mins (plus 2 hours
soaking time for the lentils, and 15–30
mins resting time for the pastry dough)
COOKING TIME: 30 mins (plus 30 mins for
the lentils)
SERVES 4–6

METHOD

1 Drain the lentils. Boil fast in fresh water
for 10 minutes. Then cover and simmer
for 20 minutes. Drain and reserve the
stock.
2 Meanwhile, put the potatoes in a pan,
cover with water, simmer until just tender,
then drain and leave to cool slightly.
3 Heat the oil in a pan and fry the onion,
cumin seeds and garlic for 5 minutes.
Sprinkle over the curry powder and add
the lentils and potatoes. Cook for 2–3
minutes. Pour on the stock and soya sauce.
Cook gently for 5 minutes, then cool.
4 For the pastry, combine the flour and
fat, then add the chilli powder. Sprinkle
on 3–4 tbsp (45–60ml) water, form a
dough, adding extra water if necessary to
make the dough moist. Cover and leave to
rest for 15–30 minutes.
5 Roll out the pastry to a 12-inch (30cm)
square. Place the cooled filling in a
diamond shape in the centre, leaving a
triangle of pastry bare at each corner.
6 Draw up the two front corners, dampen
the edges, and seal them together over the
filling. Repeat with the two back corners.
7 Place on a baking tray, glaze with milk.
Bake in a preheated oven at Gas Mark 6,
400°F, 200°C for 30 minutes. Serve the
samosa hot or cold.

*CLOCKWISE FROM TOP: Giant wholemeal samosa ; Red beans and olives (see p.50);
Butter beans au gratin (see p.50); Haricot beans with apple and cider (see p.50)*

RED BEANS AND OLIVES

INGREDIENTS

■ 8oz (250g) red kidney beans, soaked
■ 2oz (50g) small wholemeal pasta shells
■ 2 tsp (10ml) olive oil
■ 2 onions, chopped
■ 2 cloves garlic, crushed
■ 4oz (125g) button mushrooms
■ 1 tbsp (15ml) chopped fresh rosemary
■ 12 black olives, stoned and sliced
■ 1 tbsp (15ml) chopped capers
■ 2 tbsp (30ml) lemon juice
■ 1 tbsp (15ml) cider vinegar
■ 1 tbsp (15ml) tomato purée

Illustrated on page 49

Red kidney beans and black olives make a delicious combination.

PREPARATION TIME: 25 mins (plus 10–12 hours soaking time)

COOKING TIME: 10 mins (plus 40 mins for the beans)

SERVES 4

METHOD

1 Drain the beans. Cover with fresh water, bring to the boil and boil fast for 10 minutes. Reduce the heat, cover and simmer for 30 minutes, then drain.
2 Cook the pasta shells in boiling water for 5 minutes. Drain.
3 Heat the oil in a large pan and fry the onion and garlic for 5 minutes. Add the beans, mushrooms and rosemary, cover and cook for 5 minutes. Stir in the pasta shells, olives, capers, lemon juice and cider vinegar. Dissolve the tomato purée in ¼ pint (150ml) of water and pour over the beans. Cover and cook gently for 10 minutes. Serve hot or cold.

BUTTER BEANS AU GRATIN

INGREDIENTS

■ 8oz (250g) butter beans, soaked
■ 2 tsp (10ml) sunflower oil
■ 6oz (175g) mushrooms, sliced
■ 2 large leeks, sliced
■ 1 tbsp (15ml) wholemeal flour
■ ¼ tsp chilli powder
■ 1 tsp (5ml) paprika
■ ½ pint (300ml) butter bean stock
■ 2 tsp (10ml) thyme
■ 2 tsp (10ml) sage
■ 1 tsp (5ml) yeast extract
■ 2 tbsp (30ml) medium oatmeal

Illustrated on page 49

Serve this satisfying bean casserole hot with jacket potatoes and steamed carrots.

PREPARATION TIME: 30 mins (plus 10–12 hours soaking time)

COOKING TIME: 30 mins (plus 1 hour)

SERVES 4

METHOD

1 Drain the beans, cover with fresh water. Boil fast for 10 minutes. Reduce the heat, cover and simmer for 45–50 minutes.
2 Heat the oil in a large pan and gently fry the mushrooms and leeks for 10 minutes. Sprinkle the flour, chilli powder and paprika over the top. Cook for 2–3 minutes. Add the beans, stock and herbs. Cover and cook gently for 15 minutes.
3 Dissolve the yeast extract in 2 tbsp (30ml) boiling water. Add to the bean mixture. Place in an ovenproof dish, sprinkle with the oatmeal and brown under a preheated grill.

HARICOT BEANS WITH APPLE AND CIDER

INGREDIENTS

■ 8oz (250g) haricot beans, soaked
■ 2 tsp (10ml) sunflower oil
■ 1 onion, chopped
■ 1lb (500g) carrots, finely sliced
■ 2 tsp (10ml) fresh basil
■ 2 tsp (10ml) fresh marjoram
■ ½ pint (300ml) dry cider
■ 2 eating apples, diced
■ 4oz (125g) pineapple flesh, diced
■ 4oz (125g) black grapes, halved

Illustrated on page 49

This casserole is good hot or cold, served with a fresh green salad and a garnish of marjoram. The cider enhances the fruity flavour, while the herbs offset the beans and vegetables.

PREPARATION TIME: 40 mins (plus 10–12 hours soaking time)

COOKING TIME: 25 mins (plus 50 mins for the beans)

SERVES 4

METHOD

1 Drain the beans. Put into a saucepan with fresh water. Bring to the boil and boil fast for 10 minutes. Reduce the heat, cover and simmer for 40 minutes or until tender. Drain well.
2 Heat the oil in a large pan and fry the onion for 5 minutes. Add the carrots, beans, basil and marjoram and cook for 5 minutes. Add the cider, cover and simmer for 10 minutes.
3 Add the apples, pineapple and deseeded grapes. Continue cooking for 2–3 minutes. Serve hot or cold.

FROM TOP: Quick red lentils; Haricot beans and tomato sauce (see p.52); Curried chick peas (see p.52)

QUICK RED LENTILS

INGREDIENTS

- 8oz (250g) red split lentils
- 1 onion, finely chopped
- 1 clove garlic, crushed
- 2 sticks celery, finely chopped
- 1 tsp (5ml) ground cumin
- 1 tsp (5ml) garam masala
- ¼ tsp chilli powder
- 1 tsp (5ml) turmeric
- 1 bay leaf
- 1 pint (600ml) water
- 2 tsp (10ml) lemon juice
- 1 tbsp (15ml) soya sauce
- ½oz (15g) creamed coconut, finely chopped

TOPPING

- 2 tsp (10ml) sunflower oil
- 1 onion, sliced into fine rings

Illustrated left

Red lentils are ideal for a quick, healthy meal, and are a good base for any distinctive flavour. Here they are subtly spiced, then topped with crisp-fried onion rings. Serve with brown rice or steamed broccoli, and garnish with lemon wedges. If you want to reduce the fat content, leave out the fried onion rings. If you are using lentils that are not ready-prepared, remember to pick over for stones.

PREPARATION TIME: 10 mins
COOKING TIME: 25 mins
SERVES 4

METHOD

1 Wash the lentils. Put them into a large pan with the onion, garlic, celery, cumin, garam masala, chilli powder, turmeric, bay leaf and fresh water. Bring to the boil, cover the pan and simmer gently for 20–25 minutes until the liquid has been absorbed.

2 Remove the bay leaf, beat the lentil mixture into a smooth paste with a wooden spoon. Add the lemon juice, soya sauce and creamed coconut. Check the seasoning.

3 For the topping, heat the oil in a frying pan and quickly fry the onion rings until browned, taking care that they do not burn.

4 Serve the lentils hot, topped with the crisp onion rings.

HARICOT BEANS AND TOMATO SAUCE

INGREDIENTS

- 8oz (250g) haricot beans, soaked
- 2 tsp (10ml) sunflower oil
- 1 large onion, chopped
- 1 clove garlic, crushed
- 2 medium carrots, grated
- 1 dessert apple, cored and grated
- 14oz (400g) can of chopped tomatoes
- 2 tbsp (30ml) tomato purée
- 1 tsp (5ml) paprika
- pinch chilli powder
- 1 bay leaf
- 1 tbsp (15ml) soya sauce
- 1 tbsp (15ml) apple juice or honey
- 3 fl oz (75ml) water

Illustrated on page 51

This fruity recipe has a rich tomato sauce to offset the creaminess of the beans. Serve with a green salad.

PREPARATION TIME: 20 mins (plus 10–12 hours soaking time)

COOKING TIME: 40 mins (plus 50 mins for the beans)

SERVES 4

METHOD

1 Drain the beans. Cover with fresh water, bring to the boil and boil fast for 10 minutes. Reduce the heat, cover and simmer for 40 minutes. Drain and set aside.

2 Heat the oil in a pan and gently fry the onion and garlic for about 5 minutes. Add the beans and cook for 2–3 minutes.

3 Add the carrots, apple, tomatoes, tomato purée, paprika, chilli powder, bay leaf, soya sauce and apple juice or honey.

4 Bring to the boil, cover and simmer gently for 30–40 minutes, adding a little water if the mixture seems dry. Remove the bay leaf, check the seasoning and serve the beans hot.

CURRIED CHICK PEAS

INGREDIENTS

- 6oz (175g) chick peas, soaked
- 2 tsp (10ml) sunflower oil
- 2 onions, chopped
- 2 cloves garlic, crushed
- 1 tsp (5ml) cumin seeds
- 8oz (250g) potatoes, cut into pieces
- 1 tsp (5ml) ground cumin
- 1 tsp (5ml) ground coriander
- 1 tsp (5ml) turmeric
- ¼ tsp chilli powder
- 1oz (25g) raisins
- 1oz (25g) blanched almonds, chopped
- salt and pepper

Illustrated on page 51

Traditionally known as Channa Dhal. Serve with brown rice and a natural yogurt, cucumber and mint salad. Garnish with coriander.

PREPARATION TIME: 15 mins (plus 10–12 hours soaking time)

COOKING TIME: 35 mins (plus 50 mins for the chick peas)

SERVES 4

METHOD

1 Drain the chick peas. Cover with fresh water, bring to the boil and boil fast for 10 minutes. Reduce the heat, cover and simmer for 40 minutes. Drain and reserve the stock.

2 Heat the oil in a pan and fry the onion, garlic and cumin seeds for 5 minutes. Add the potatoes, chick peas and spices and cook for 3–4 minutes.

3 Pour over ¾ pint (450ml) reserved stock. Cover and simmer for 25–30 minutes. Add the raisins, cook for a further 3–4 minutes, stir in the almonds, check the seasoning and serve hot.

FROM LEFT: Aubergine and butter bean biryani; Crunchy casserole with chick peas

CRUNCHY CASSEROLE WITH CHICK PEAS

INGREDIENTS

- 4oz (125g) chick peas, soaked
- 2 medium carrots cut into strips
- 1 small head fennel, sliced thinly
- 1 tsp (5ml) caraway seeds
- 2 oz (50g) French beans, trimmed
- 1 small red pepper, sliced thinly
- 2 tbsp (30ml) fresh parsley
- ¼ pint (150ml) chick pea stock or water
- 3 tbsp (45ml) natural yogurt
- 1 tbsp (15ml) mayonnaise
- 1 clove garlic, crushed

Illustrated above

This is a very healthy and filling hot or cold accompaniment to a main dish.
PREPARATION TIME: 10 mins (plus 10–12 hours soaking time)
COOKING TIME: 15 mins (plus 50 mins for the beans)
SERVES 4

METHOD

1 Drain the chick peas and boil fast in fresh water for 10 minutes. Simmer for 40 minutes. Drain well, reserving the stock.
2 Put the chick peas into a casserole. Cover with thin strips of carrots and fennel. Sprinkle with caraway seeds. Layer the French beans and red pepper strips on top. Sprinkle with the fresh parsley. Pour over the stock or water. Cover and bake in a preheated oven at Gas Mark 4, 350°F, 180°C for 15 minutes. Pour on the dressing of yogurt, mayonnaise and garlic mixed together and serve hot or cold.

AUBERGINE AND BUTTER BEAN BIRYANI

INGREDIENTS

- 3oz (75g) butter beans, soaked
- 2 tsp (10ml) sunflower oil
- 1 tsp (5ml) poppy seeds
- 1 tsp (5ml) mustard seeds
- 8oz (250g) long-grain brown rice
- ¼ tsp chilli powder
- 1 tsp (5ml) turmeric
- 1 tsp (5ml) garam masala
- 1 tsp (5ml) ground coriander
- 2 tbsp (30ml) cold water
- 1 medium aubergine, diced
- 1 large red pepper, deseeded and cut into strips
- 14oz (400g) can of tomatoes
- cold water or butter bean stock
- 1 tbsp (15ml) soya sauce
- 3 tbsp (45ml) natural yogurt

Illustrated left

A biryani is an Indian-style paella. Here, butter beans and aubergines are combined with mildly spiced rice to make a delicious, well-balanced meal. If you prefer to use canned butter beans, double the quantity, and, to prevent them becoming too soft, add to the biryani 10 minutes from the end of the cooking time.
PREPARATION TIME: 25 mins (plus 10–12 hours soaking time)
COOKING TIME: 30–40 mins (plus 1 hour for the beans)
SERVES 4

METHOD

1 Drain the beans. Put in a saucepan and cover with fresh water. Bring to the boil and boil fast for 10 minutes. Reduce the heat, cover and simmer for 50 minutes or until just tender. Drain well, reserving the stock.
2 Heat the oil in a large pan. Gently cook the poppy and mustard seeds until they begin to pop. Add the rice and continue cooking gently for 3–4 minutes.
3 In a separate bowl mix together the chilli powder, turmeric, garam masala and coriander, adding 2 tbsp (30ml) cold water to make a paste. Pour the paste over the rice, then add the aubergine, red pepper and butter beans, coating them well. Cook gently for 3–4 minutes.
4 Drain the tomatoes, reserving the juice, and add them to the rice mixture. Make the juice up to 1 pint (600ml) with the water or bean stock and pour on to the rice. Add the soya sauce.
5 Cover and simmer for 30–40 minutes until the rice is cooked and most of the liquid is absorbed. Stir in the yogurt. Check the seasoning and serve hot.

VEGETABLE AND LENTIL COTTAGE PIE

INGREDIENTS

- 8oz (250g) brown lentils
- 2 bay leaves
- 2 tsp (10ml) sunflower oil
- 1 onion, finely chopped
- 4oz (125g) carrots, finely chopped
- 3 sticks celery, diced
- 2 tsp (10ml) paprika
- 1 tsp (5ml) chopped fresh marjoram
- 1 tsp (5ml) chopped fresh sage
- 1 tbsp (15ml) tomato purée
- 1 tbsp (15ml) soya sauce
- 1 tsp (5ml) yeast extract
- ½ pint (300ml) lentil stock or water
- salt and pepper
- 1lb (500g) potatoes, chopped
- ½oz (15g) margarine
- 2 tbsp (30ml) skimmed milk
- 2 large tomatoes, sliced
- 2 tsp (10ml) sesame seeds

GARNISH

- sprig of sage
- sprig of marjoram

Illustrated right

Continental or brown lentils are used here to create a simple yet substantial family meal. If you are using lentils that are not ready-prepared, remember to rinse them well and pick over for stones. Try serving with lightly steamed green vegetables and a tomato sauce, and garnish with sage and marjoram.

PREPARATION TIME: 1 hour
COOKING TIME: 30 mins
SERVES 4

METHOD

1 Wash the lentils. Cover with plenty of cold water in a large saucepan. Add the bay leaves, bring to the boil, cover the pan and simmer gently for 25 minutes or until the lentils are soft. Drain well and reserve the stock. Remove the bay leaves and set aside.
2 Heat the oil in a large saucepan and fry the onion, carrots and celery for 5 minutes.
3 Add the cooked lentils, the paprika, marjoram and sage together with the tomato purée, soya sauce, yeast extract and lentil stock. Cover and simmer gently for 15–20 minutes. Check the seasoning.
4 Meanwhile, boil the potatoes until cooked. Drain, add the margarine and milk, and mash well.
5 Put the lentil mixture into the base of a large casserole. Cover with sliced tomatoes. Top with the mashed potato. Sprinkle over the seasame seeds. and bake in a preheated oven at Gas Mark 4, 350°F, 180°C for 30 minutes. Add the garnish of herbs and serve hot.

FROM TOP: Savoury crumble; Baked tomatoes; Vegetable and lentil cottage pie

SAVOURY CRUMBLE

INGREDIENTS

- 2 tsp (10ml) sunflower oil
- 1 onion, chopped
- 4oz (125g) mushrooms, sliced if large
- 4oz (125g) carrots, sliced
- 1 small cauliflower, cut into florets
- 2 tsp (10ml) chopped fresh rosemary
- 1 tbsp (15ml) wholemeal flour
- ½ pint (300ml) water
- 1 tsp (5ml) yeast extract
- 2 tbsp (30ml) boiling water
- ¼ tsp black pepper

TOPPING

- 3oz (75g) porridge or jumbo oats
- 1oz (25g) blanched almonds, chopped
- 1 tbsp (15ml) sunflower oil

Illustrated left

This mixed vegetable casserole is made more unusual and more nutritious by a nutty crumble topping. Various combinations of vegetables can be used according to season and choice. Jumbo oats in the topping give a very crunchy texture, but the smaller porridge oats can be used instead. Serve with a garnish of rosemary.

PREPARATION TIME: 40 mins
COOKING TIME: 30 mins
SERVES 4

METHOD

1 Heat the oil over a moderate heat in a large frying pan and fry the onion, mushrooms, carrots and cauliflower. Cover and cook for 10 minutes, stirring frequently.
2 Sprinkle on the rosemary and flour and cook for 2–3 minutes. Pour on the water, bring to the boil and simmer gently for 5 minutes. Stir in the yeast extract (dissolved in the boiling water) and the pepper. Put the mixture into a casserole or into an ovenproof dish.
3 For the topping, mix together the oats, almonds and oil. Sprinkle on top of the vegetables.
4 Bake in a preheated oven at Gas Mark 4, 350°F, 180°C for 30 minutes. Serve hot.

BAKED TOMATOES

INGREDIENTS

- 8 large, firm tomatoes
- 2 tsp (10ml) olive oil
- 1 onion, finely chopped
- 4oz (125g) mushrooms, finely chopped
- 2oz (50g) blanched almonds, chopped
- 2 tsp (10ml) chopped fresh thyme
- pinch chilli powder
- 4oz (125g) wholemeal breadcrumbs
- 2 tsp (10ml) soya sauce
- ½ tsp black pepper
- 3 fl oz (75ml) water

Illustrated left

Served hot or cold, these savoury tomatoes make a simple, appetizing meal. Garnish with lemon and thyme.

PREPARATION TIME: 30 mins
COOKING TIME: 25 mins
SERVES 4

METHOD

1 Slice the tops off the tomatoes, scoop out and reserve the flesh and seeds. Put the tomato cases into an ovenproof dish.
2 Heat the oil and fry the onion for 4–5 minutes. Add the mushrooms, almonds, thyme and chilli powder. Cover and cook gently for another 7–10 minutes. Add the breadcrumbs, tomato flesh and seeds, soya sauce and pepper. Check the seasoning.
3 Stuff the tomato cases and replace the tops. Pour the water into the dish. Bake in a preheated oven at Gas Mark 5, 375°F, 190°C for 25 minutes.

CHINESE BAKE WITH WATERCRESS SAUCE

INGREDIENTS

- 1½lb (750g) Chinese leaves
- 8oz (250g) cottage cheese with chives
- ¼ tsp black pepper
- 1oz (25g) margarine
- 1 bunch watercress, chopped
- 1 small onion, chopped
- 1 clove garlic, chopped
- 2 tbsp (30ml) grated Parmesan cheese

Illustrated left

Serve with potatoes and a carrot salad for a balanced, low-calorie meal.

PREPARATION TIME: 35 mins
COOKING TIME: 25 mins
SERVES 4

METHOD

1 Cut the leafy part from the Chinese leaves, and steam the stems gently for 3–4 minutes. Put the cottage cheese into a large casserole dish, sprinkle with black pepper and cover with the stems.
2 Melt the margarine slowly. Add the chopped leaves, watercress, onion and garlic. Cover and cook gently for 7–8 minutes. Cool slightly, then purée until smooth.
3 Pour the watercress mixture over the cottage cheese and stems. Sprinkle over the Parmesan cheese and bake in a preheated oven at Gas Mark 4, 350°F, 180°C for 25 minutes. Serve hot.

Chinese bake with watercress sauce

Baked Spanish omelette

BAKED SPANISH OMELETTE

INGREDIENTS

■ 10oz (300g) potatoes, diced
■ 4oz (125g) carrots, diced
■ 4oz (125g) sweetcorn, fresh, frozen or canned
■ ½ tsp sunflower oil
■ 1 small courgette, thinly sliced
■ 1 small red pepper, cut into thin strips
■ 12 black olives
■ 4 eggs, well beaten
■ 7 fl oz (200ml) skimmed milk
■ 1 tsp (5ml) chopped fresh thyme
■ ½ tsp paprika
■ 1 clove garlic, crushed
■ salt and black pepper
■ 2 large tomatoes, thinly sliced
■ 1½oz (40g) grated Cheddar cheese

Illustrated above

This recipe is like a quiche without the pastry case, which keeps the fat and calorie content down. Vary the vegetables according to season.

PREPARATION TIME: 30 mins
COOKING TIME: 45 mins
SERVES 4

METHOD

1 Cover the potatoes and carrots with plenty of water, bring to the boil and simmer gently for 10 minutes. If using fresh sweetcorn, add to the potatoes and carrots for the last 4–5 minutes. Drain and set aside.
2 Lightly oil an 8-inch (20cm) round dish. Put in the potatoes, carrots and sweetcorn. Cover with slices of courgette and pepper, and the stoned olives.
3 Mix together the eggs, milk, thyme, paprika and garlic. Season and then pour over the vegetable mixture. Cover with slices of tomato and grated cheese.
4 Bake in a preheated oven at Gas Mark 5, 375°F, 190°C for 45 minutes or until golden brown and set. Serve hot.

STUFFED AUBERGINES WITH APRICOTS

INGREDIENTS

■ 2 small aubergines
■ 8oz (250g) red split lentils
■ 2 tsp (10ml) olive oil
■ 1 small onion, finely chopped
■ ½ tsp ground cumin
■ ½ tsp ground coriander
■ 3oz (75g) dried apricots, chopped
■ 2 tbsp (30ml) apple juice
■ 1 tbsp (15ml) soya sauce
■ 3 tbsp (45ml) lentil stock or water

Illustrated below

Serve this healthy version of a traditional Turkish dish with a tomato sauce and a crisp green pepper and lettuce salad.
PREPARATION TIME: 45 mins
COOKING TIME: 45 mins
SERVES 4

METHOD

1 Halve the aubergines and scoop out.
2 Cover the lentils with water. Bring to the boil, cover and simmer for 15–20 minutes. Drain, and reserve any excess liquid.
3 Heat the oil over a moderate heat and gently cook the onion, cumin and coriander for 5 minutes. Stir in the aubergine flesh and drained lentils and cook for 5–8 minutes. Add the apricots, apple juice, soya sauce and the stock or water. Cook for a further 5 minutes. Check the seasoning.
4 Fill the aubergine shells with the mixture. Cover and bake in a preheated oven at Gas Mark 5, 375°F, 190°C for 45 minutes.

Stuffed aubergines with apricots

FROM TOP: Cheesy leek and potato casserole; Mixed vegetable curry

CHEESY LEEK AND POTATO CASSEROLE

INGREDIENTS

■ 1lb (500g) leeks, cut into ¾ inch (1½cm) slices
■ 1lb (500g) potatoes, cut into ¼ inch (5mm) slices
■ 1½oz (40g) margarine
■ 1oz (25g) wholemeal flour
■ ½ pint (300ml) skimmed milk
■ ½ tsp mustard powder or Dijon mustard
■ ¼ tsp black pepper
■ 2oz (50g) Cheddar cheese, grated

Illustrated above

Steam the leeks carefully so that they remain slightly crunchy. Use a mature cheese for maximum flavour.

PREPARATION TIME: 40 mins
COOKING TIME: 25 mins
SERVES 4

METHOD

1 Steam the leeks over a large pan of simmering water for 8 minutes.
2 Meanwhile, cover the potato slices with water. Bring to the boil and simmer gently for 10 minutes. Drain well.
3 Melt the margarine, add the flour and cook gently, stirring, for 2–3 minutes. Remove from the heat, gradually stir in the milk. Return to the heat and bring to the boil, stirring constantly. Cook gently for 2–3 minutes. Stir in the mustard and pepper.
4 Layer the leeks and potato in a casserole or ovenproof dish. Pour the sauce over the top and sprinkle with grated cheese. Bake in a preheated oven at Gas Mark 4, 350°F, 180°C for 25 minutes until golden brown. Serve hot.

MIXED VEGETABLE CURRY

INGREDIENTS

■ 2 tsp (10ml) sunflower oil
■ 1 tsp (5ml) cumin seeds
■ 1 tsp (5ml) coriander seeds
■ 1 large onion, finely chopped
■ 3 cloves garlic, crushed
■ 1 tsp (5ml) garam masala
■ ¼ tsp chilli powder
■ 1 medium potato, finely diced
■ 1 parsnip, cut into small chunks
■ 1 courgette, sliced
■ 1 green pepper, deseeded and cut into strips
■ 1 small aubergine, diced
■ 2 tbsp (30ml) wholemeal flour
■ 14oz (400g) can of chopped tomatoes
■ ¼ pint (150ml) water or stock
■ 1½ tbsp (25ml) yogurt
■ 1 tbsp (15ml) soya sauce

Illustrated left

This mixed vegetable curry is good served with plain brown rice and poppadums. If made a day in advance, the flavours of the curry have more time to develop. If you do not have the various spices, use 1–2 tbsp (15–30ml) mild curry powder.

PREPARATION TIME: 30 mins
COOKING TIME: 40 mins
SERVES 4

METHOD

1 Heat the oil over a moderate heat in a large pan. Gently cook the cumin and coriander seeds for 4–5 minutes until the seeds are turning brown. Add the onion, garlic, garam masala and chilli powder, and continue cooking gently for a further 5 minutes.
2 Add the potato, parsnip, courgette, green pepper and aubergine to the pan. Continue cooking for 5 minutes, stirring well to ensure that the vegetables are well coated in spices. Sprinkle over the flour and cook for 2–3 minutes.
3 Add the tomatoes and their juice, together with the water or stock. Cover and simmer for 40 minutes, stirring occasionally and adding a little extra water or stock if necessary.
4 When the vegetables are tender, add the yogurt and soya sauce. Check the seasoning and serve hot.

FROM TOP: *Cheese and walnut loaf; Cauliflower and almond bake*

CHEESE AND WALNUT LOAF

INGREDIENTS

■ 8oz (250g) cottage cheese
■ 2oz (50g) walnuts, ground
■ 2 tsp (10ml) wholegrain mustard
■ 4oz (125g) wholemeal breadcrumbs
■ 8 black peppercorns, crushed
■ 2 eggs, beaten

GARNISH
■ frisé (curly endive)

Illustrated above

This nutty loaf is ideal for serving with salads, green vegetables or with a tomato or mushroom sauce. For a smoother texture, try using skimmed milk soft cheese (quark) instead of cottage cheese. Garnish with frisé (curly endive).

PREPARATION TIME: 10 mins
COOKING TIME: 30–40 mins
SERVES 4

METHOD

1 Combine the cottage cheese, walnuts, mustard, breadcrumbs, peppercorns and eggs in a large bowl and mix well.
2 Lightly oil a 1lb (500g) loaf tin or a small casserole. Put the mixture into the tin or dish.
3 Bake in a preheated oven at Gas Mark 4, 350°F, 180°C for 30–40 minutes until golden brown. Serve hot or cold.

CAULIFLOWER AND ALMOND BAKE

INGREDIENTS

■ 1 medium cauliflower, cut into florets
■ 2 tsp (10ml) sunflower oil
■ 1 onion, chopped
■ 1 clove garlic, crushed
■ 2oz (50g) almonds, roughly chopped
■ 2oz (50g) ground almonds
■ 1 tbsp (15ml) soya sauce
■ 1 tsp (5ml) chopped fresh marjoram

GARNISH
■ lemon slices
■ fresh parsley

Illustrated left

An interesting and healthy alternative to cauliflower cheese, this recipe combines lightly steamed cauliflower with almonds and herbs. Serve with brown rice or jacket potatoes and a green salad; garnish with lemon slices and parsley.

PREPARATION TIME: 35 mins
COOKING TIME: 30 mins
SERVES 4

METHOD

1 Put the cauliflower into a steamer or colander over a pan of boiling water and steam gently for 10–15 minutes, until the cauliflower is just tender. Reserve the water and make up to ½ pint (300ml) with fresh water. Put the cauliflower on to the base of a large ovenproof dish.
2 Heat the oil in a pan and gently fry the onion and garlic for 5 minutes. Add the almonds and cook gently for a further 4–5 minutes. Spoon over the cauliflower.
3 In a blender or food processor, mix together the ground almonds, cauliflower water, soya sauce and marjoram. Pour over the cauliflower. Bake in a preheated oven at Gas Mark 4, 350°F, 180°C for 25–30 minutes. Serve hot.

Hazelnut loaf with mushroom and pepper sauce

HAZELNUT LOAF WITH MUSHROOM AND PEPPER SAUCE

INGREDIENTS

■ 4oz (125g) hazelnuts, ground
■ 4oz (125g) wholemeal breadcrumbs
■ 2 tsp (10ml) sunflower oil
■ 1 onion, finely chopped
■ 2 large carrots, grated
■ 2 sticks celery, finely chopped
■ 1 tsp (5ml) chopped fresh sage
■ 1 tsp (5ml) chopped fresh thyme
■ 1 tsp (5ml) yeast extract
■ ¼ pint (150ml) boiling water
■ 1 tbsp (15ml) soya sauce
■ 1 egg, beaten
■ 3 large tomatoes, sliced
■ 3 tbsp (45ml) chopped fresh parsley

SAUCE
■ 1oz (25g) margarine
■ 2 tsp (10ml) chopped fresh dill
■ pinch chilli powder
■ 4oz (125g) mushrooms, finely chopped
■ 1 small green pepper, deseeded and finely chopped
■ 1oz (25g) wholemeal flour
■ ½ pint (300ml) skimmed milk
■ 2 tsp (10ml) soya sauce

Illustrated left

This nut loaf makes a nutritious and satisfying meal, whether you serve it hot in the light, creamy sauce with steamed vegetables, or cold with a salad. The central layer of herbs and juicy tomatoes and the spicy mushroom and pepper sauce lend a piquant flavour and moisten the texture of the loaf. Garnish the loaf with a sprig of sage, and the sauce with sprigs of dill.
PREPARATION TIME: 25 mins
COOKING TIME: 40 mins
SERVES 4

METHOD

1 Mix the hazelnuts and breadcrumbs together in a large bowl.
2 Heat the oil in a pan and gently fry the onion, carrots and celery for 5 minutes until soft. Add to the nut and breadcrumb mixture, together with the sage and thyme.
3 Dissolve the yeast extract in the water, and add to the bowl with the soya sauce. Mix in the beaten egg.
4 Put about half the nut mixture into the base of a lightly oiled 1lb (500g) loaf tin. Cover with the sliced tomatoes and parsley. Top with the rest of the nut mixture.
5 Bake in a preheated oven at Gas Mark 4, 350°F, 180°C for 35–40 minutes. Serve hot or cold.
6 For the sauce, melt the margarine in a small pan, add the dill and chilli powder, mushrooms and green pepper. Cover and cook gently for 10 minutes.
7 Stir in the flour and cook for 2–3 minutes. Remove from the heat and gradually stir in the milk. Bring to the boil, stirring continuously, and simmer gently for 3–4 minutes. Add the soya sauce, stirring it in well, and serve.

COLOURFUL BEAN LOAF WITH CARROT SAUCE

INGREDIENTS

■ 6oz (175g) red kidney beans, soaked
■ 2 tsp (10ml) olive oil
■ 1 large onion, finely chopped
■ 2 cloves garlic, crushed
■ 4oz (125g) carrot, grated
■ 6oz (175g) sweetcorn kernels, fresh, frozen or canned
■ 1½ tsp (7½ml) dill seeds
■ 4 tsp (20ml) chopped fresh marjoram
■ 4oz (125g) porridge oats
■ 1 egg
■ 2 tbsp (30ml) soya sauce
■ ¼ tsp black pepper
■ 3–4 tbsp (45–60ml) bean stock
■ 1 small red pepper, cut into thin strips
■ 1 small green pepper, cut into thin strips

SAUCE
■ 2 tsp (10ml) olive oil
■ 1 large onion, finely chopped
■ 8oz (250g) carrots, sliced
■ ¾ pint (450ml) vegetable stock or water
■ 1 tsp (5ml) yeast extract
■ 4 tbsp (60ml) orange juice
■ 2 tbsp (30ml) chopped fresh parsley
■ salt and pepper

Illustrated on page 60

This loaf is delicious served hot with a carrot sauce, or cold.
PREPARATION TIME: 30 mins (plus 10–12 hours soaking time)
COOKING TIME: 40 mins (plus 40 mins for the beans)
SERVES 4–6

METHOD

1 Drain the beans. Place in a saucepan and cover with fresh water. Bring to the boil and boil fast for 10 minutes. Reduce the heat, cover and simmer for 30 minutes, or until the beans are soft. Drain, reserving the stock, and mash the beans while still warm.
2 Heat the oil and gently fry the onion and garlic for 5–7 minutes. Add the carrot and sweetcorn. If using frozen sweetcorn, defrost first; if using fresh sweetcorn, cook in boiling water for 5 minutes first. Rinse canned sweetcorn before using. Cook for a further 5 minutes.
3 Stir in the dill seeds, marjoram, mashed beans and porridge oats and mix well. Beat together the egg, soya sauce and black pepper. Add to the bean mixture. Add enough stock to make a moist consistency.
4 Lightly oil a 2lb (1kg) loaf tin. Lay half the strips of red and green pepper along the base. Top with half the bean mixture. Then lay the rest of the pepper strips on top, finishing with the bean mixture.
5 Bake in a preheated oven at Gas Mark 4, 350°F, 180°C for 35–40 minutes. Leave in the tin for 5 minutes before turning out.
6 For the sauce, heat the oil in a pan and gently fry the onion for 5–7 minutes. Add the carrots and cook for 2–3 minutes.
7 Pour on the water or vegetable stock, add the yeast extract. Bring to the boil, cover and simmer for 10 minutes, until the carrots are tender. Cool slightly.
8 Purée the vegetables until smooth. Return to the pan, add the orange juice and parsley. Warm through gently, check the seasoning and serve on top of the loaf.

FROM TOP: *Colourful bean loaf with carrot sauce (see p.59); Almond wheel*

ALMOND WHEEL

INGREDIENTS

- 2 tsp (10ml) olive oil
- 1 large onion, finely chopped
- 1 clove garlic, crushed
- 8oz (250g) long-grain brown rice
- 3oz (75g) blanched almonds, chopped
- 1 yellow pepper, deseeded and chopped
- 2oz (50g) raisins
- 1 tsp (5ml) ground cinnamon
- grated rind of 1 orange
- 3 tbsp (45ml) orange juice
- 1 tbsp (15ml) soya sauce
- 1 egg

FILLING

- 12oz (375g) tomatoes, chopped
- 6oz (175g) French beans, trimmed
- 1 clove garlic, crushed
- 1 tsp (5ml) chopped fresh basil
- 2 tbsp (30ml) chopped fresh parsley

Illustrated left

This summery combination is ideal for a special occasion or buffet. Make sure the vegetables are lightly cooked and still crunchy.

PREPARATION TIME: 1 hour
COOKING TIME: 30 mins
SERVES 4

METHOD

1 Heat the oil in a large pan and gently fry the onion and garlic for 5 minutes. Add the rice and almonds, and cook gently for 3–4 minutes until the almonds begin to turn golden brown.
2 Add the yellow pepper, raisins and cinnamon and cook for 2–3 minutes. Stir in the orange rind, juice and 1 pint (600ml) boiling water. Bring to the boil, cover and simmer for 30 minutes. Drain and stir in the soya sauce and beaten egg.
3 Lightly oil an 8-inch (20cm) ring mould and press the rice mixture into the mould. Bake in a preheated oven at Gas Mark 4, 350°F, 180°C for 30 minutes, or until firm.
4 For the filling, gently cook the tomatoes for 5 minutes. Stir in the French beans, garlic, basil and parsley. Cover and cook for 8–10 minutes. Add a little water if the mixture seems dry.
5 Turn out the rice. Fill the centre of the ring with the tomatoes and beans. Serve hot or cold.

USING A RING MOULD

*T*he shape of a dish can often be an important part of its appeal, just as much as its colour, texture and aroma. Ring moulds are used to make circular loaves and cakes, as well as mousses and jellies. If you do not have a ring mould, an upside down mixing bowl and a loose-bottomed cake tin will do just as well.

1 *If using a mould, brush the sides with a little oil, tightly pack in the mixture and bake.*

2 *If making your own mould, line a cake tin and place a Pyrex bowl in the centre. Brush with a little oil.*

3 *When baked, turn out on to a plate, and remove the cake tin, greaseproof paper and finally the bowl.*

SHARP RICE WITH MILD SAUCE

INGREDIENTS

- 1 tsp (5ml) sunflower oil
- 1 onion, finely chopped
- 1 small green pepper, deseeded and diced
- 8oz (250g) long-grain brown rice
- 1 pint (600ml) boiling water
- 1 tsp (5ml) chopped fresh thyme
- grated rind of 1 large lemon
- ¼ tsp salt

SAUCE
- ½ tsp sunflower oil
- 2 large leeks, finely chopped
- 2oz (50g) unsalted cashew nuts
- 2oz (50g) unsalted cashew nuts, ground
- ¼ pint (150ml) water
- 1 tbsp (15ml) soya sauce

Illustrated on page 62

This unusual dish has a tangy base of lemon-flavoured rice and is topped with a smooth leek and cashew nut sauce. The contrasts of flavour and texture make it an interesting recipe for a dinner party, served with a frisé salad, steamed spinach or sorrel.

PREPARATION TIME: 25 mins
COOKING TIME: 30 mins
SERVES 4

METHOD

1 Heat the oil over a moderate heat in a large pan and gently fry the onion for 10 minutes. Add the pepper and rice and cook for a further 5 minutes.
2 Pour on the water and stir in the thyme and lemon rind. Bring to the boil, cover and simmer for 30 minutes, or until the rice is cooked and the liquid absorbed. Season with the salt to taste.
3 For the sauce, heat the remaining oil in a large pan and gently fry the leeks and the whole cashews, covered, for 15 minutes until the cashews become golden brown.
4 Combine the ground cashews and water and then pour on to the leeks and cashew nuts, and warm through gently. Add a little extra water if necessary, to make a thick sauce. Add the soya sauce and check the seasoning.
5 Serve the rice hot, topped with the leek and cashew sauce.

FROM LEFT: Sharp rice with mild sauce (see p.61); Aubergine and mushroom rice; Almond and vegetable paella

ALMOND AND VEGETABLE PAELLA

INGREDIENTS

▌ 2 tsp (10ml) sunflower oil
▌ 1 onion, chopped
▌ 1 clove garlic
▌ 3oz (75g) whole almonds, blanched
▌ 6oz (175g) long-grain brown rice
▌ 1 stick celery
▌ 8oz (250g) summer green vegetables
▌ 1 small green pepper, sliced
▌ 1 tsp (5ml) cumin seeds, crushed
▌ 2 tsp (10ml) fresh marjoram
▌ 2 bay leaves
▌ 1 tbsp (15ml) soya sauce or salt and pepper
▌ 1 tbsp (15ml) lemon juice

Illustrated above

Brown rice is a good source of B vitamins and fibre, while almonds not only provide protein, but also give a creamy flavour.
PREPARATION TIME: 20 mins
COOKING TIME: 30 mins
SERVES 4

METHOD

1 Heat the oil in a large pan and fry the onion and garlic for 5 minutes. Add the almonds and rice and cook for 5 minutes. Add the chopped celery, green vegetables, green pepper, cumin seeds and marjoram. Cook gently for a further 5 minutes.
2 Stir in 2 bay leaves and 1 pint (600ml) boiling water. Bring to the boil, cover and simmer for 30 minutes until the rice is cooked and the liquid has been absorbed.
3 Add the soya sauce, or season with salt and pepper, add the lemon juice, remove the bay leaves and serve hot.

AUBERGINE AND MUSHROOM RICE

INGREDIENTS

▌ 8oz (250g) long-grain brown rice
▌ 2 tsp (10ml) olive oil
▌ 1 large onion
▌ 1 large clove garlic
▌ 12oz (375g) aubergine, diced
▌ 4oz (125g) mushrooms
▌ 2 tsp (10ml) chopped fresh marjoram
▌ 2 tsp (10ml) chopped fresh thyme
▌ 1 tsp (5ml) paprika
▌ 1oz (25g) wholemeal flour
▌ ½ pint (300ml) skimmed milk
▌ 1 tbsp (15ml) soya sauce

Illustrated above

This dish is excellent served with broccoli or tomatoes.
PREPARATION TIME: 1 hour
COOKING TIME: 30 mins
SERVES 4

METHOD

1 Place the rice in 1 pint (600ml) boiling water. Bring to the boil, cover and simmer for 25 minutes. Drain and transfer the rice to a large casserole or ovenproof dish.
2 Heat the oil and gently fry the chopped onion and garlic for 5 minutes. Add the aubergine and quartered mushrooms and cook for a further 10 minutes.
3 Add the marjoram, thyme, paprika and flour and cook for 2–3 minutes. Add the milk and simmer for 5 minutes. Add the soya sauce and check the seasoning.
4 Put the aubergine mixture on top of the rice. Cover and bake in a preheated oven at Gas Mark 4, 350°F, 180°C for 30 minutes. Serve hot.

SPINACH WITH WALNUTS

INGREDIENTS

- 2lb (1kg) fresh spinach (or 1½lb/750g frozen leaf spinach)
- 1 tbsp (15ml) sunflower oil
- 1 onion, finely chopped
- ½ tsp black pepper
- ½ tsp grated nutmeg
- ¼ pint (150ml) soured cream, smetana or natural yogurt
- 2oz (50g) wholemeal breadcrumbs
- 2oz (50g) walnuts, roughly chopped

GARNISH

- walnut halves
- fresh parsley

Illustrated right

Spinach is rich in iron and has a wonderfully strong flavour. Here it is combined with soured cream, smetana or yogurt for extra creaminess, topped with crisp walnuts and breadcrumbs, and garnished with walnut halves and parsley. You can use fresh or frozen spinach for this recipe, but fresh gives the best flavour.

PREPARATION TIME: 35 mins
COOKING TIME: 20 mins
SERVES 4

METHOD

1 Wash the spinach if using fresh, in several changes of water. Put it into a large pan with a little extra water, cover tightly and cook gently over a low heat, stirring occasionally, for about 10 minutes until the spinach has reduced and is tender.
2 Drain in a colander and then chop. If using frozen spinach, cook according to the directions on the packet. Then drain in a colander, and chop.
3 Heat 2 tsp (10ml) of the oil in a large pan over a moderate heat and gently fry the onion for 10 minutes until soft.
4 Add the cooked spinach, black pepper and nutmeg and cook for 5 minutes.
5 Remove from the heat and stir in the soured cream, smetana or yogurt. Put the spinach mixture into a casserole or ovenproof dish.
6 Mix together the breadcrumbs, chopped walnuts and the remaining 1 tsp (5ml) of oil. Sprinkle over the spinach.
7 Bake in a preheated oven at Gas Mark 4, 350°F, 180°C for 20 minutes. Serve hot garnished with walnut halves and fresh parsley.

FROM TOP: Chestnut and mushroom bake (see p.64); Spinach with walnuts

CHESTNUT AND MUSHROOM BAKE

INGREDIENTS

- 1 tsp (5ml) olive oil
- 1 clove garlic, crushed
- 6oz (175g) shallots or pickling onions, peeled, and sliced if large
- 6oz (175g) button mushrooms
- 4oz (125g) carrots, grated
- 1 stick celery, trimmed and finely shredded
- 1 tsp (5ml) chopped fresh rosemary
- 1 tsp (5ml) chopped fresh thyme
- 1 tsp (5ml) chopped fresh sage
- 1 tbsp (15ml) soya sauce
- ¼ tsp black pepper
- 10oz (283g) can whole chestnuts, finely chopped
- ½ pint (300ml) vegetable stock

Illustrated on page 63

Serve this highly flavoured nut and vegetable dish with a sharp tomato sauce (see Wholemeal spaghetti bake, page 67) and jacket potatoes or salad. Garnish with celery leaves, carrot slices and thyme.

PREPARATION TIME: 15 mins
COOKING TIME: 40 mins
SERVES 4

METHOD

1 Heat the oil in a large pan and gently fry the garlic and shallots or onions over a moderate heat for 5–7 minutes. Add the mushrooms, carrots and celery and cook for a further 7–10 minutes.
2 Add the rosemary, thyme, sage, soya sauce and black pepper. Mix the chopped chestnuts in with the herbs. Gradually add up to ½ pint (300ml) of stock until the mixture is moist.
3 Put the chestnut mixture into a casserole or oven proof dish. Bake in a preheated oven at Gas Mark 4, 350°F, 180°C for 40 minutes. Serve hot.

MAKING PASTA VERDE

INGREDIENTS

- 8oz (250g) spinach, trimmed
- ¼ pint (150ml) water
- 1lb (500g) wholemeal flour

Make red pasta by mixing 4 tbsp (60ml) of tomato purée and enough water to make ½ pint (300ml) liquid. Mix this in well with the flour.

PREPARATION TIME: 50 mins
MAKES ABOUT 1½lb (750g) pasta dough
SERVES 8

METHOD

1 Cook the spinach in ¼ pint (150ml) water, drain and press well, reserving the drained liquid. Liquidize (or chop very finely with a knife) to form a purée.
2 Make up the cooking liquid to 8 fl oz (250ml) with water. Mix with the flour and 2oz (50g) spinach purée to form a dough.

BASIC PASTA DOUGH

INGREDIENTS

- 1lb (500g) strong wholemeal flour
- 9 fl oz (275ml) water

Pasta is traditionally made from refined durum wheat flour, but wholemeal flour can be used very successfully. Choose a strong flour that is described as "100 per cent wholemeal" – preferably stoneground and made from organically grown wheat. Eggs and salt make a rich pasta dough, but for a pasta that is lower in fat, use water instead of eggs, and the salt can be left out entirely. Make the dough in large quantities and then freeze the surplus for up to 3 months.

PREPARATION TIME: 50 mins
MAKES ABOUT: 1½lb (750g) pasta dough
SERVES 8

METHOD

1 Put the flour into a mixing bowl and make a well in the centre. Pour in the water, mixing with a knife until the dough binds.
2 Mix with your hands and knead until all the flour has been incorporated (the dough will seem too dry at first).
3 Turn out on to a work surface and knead for about 10 minutes until the dough is smooth and elastic.
4 Cover the dough with clingfilm, or put into a polythene bag and leave to rest for 30 minutes before rolling out.
5 If rolling out by hand, roll out a quarter of the dough at a time on a lightly floured surface. Roll as thinly as possible. Leave to rest and dry out slightly before using.

MAKING PASTA

*P*asta can be made from different flours and moulded into different shapes and sizes. A basic dough, using wholemeal flour, is very versatile. Once made, shape it by hand or by machine.

1 Mix the flour and water using a knife.

2 Knead the dough until it is smooth and elastic.

3 Wrap in clingfilm and leave to rest before rolling out.

WHOLEWHEAT SPAGHETTI WITH WALNUT AND PARSLEY SAUCE

INGREDIENTS

- 12oz (375g) wholewheat spaghetti
- 1 tsp (5ml) lemon juice
- 6oz (175g) walnuts, finely ground
- 1 clove garlic, crushed
- ¾ pint (450ml) skimmed milk
- 3 tbsp (45ml) chopped fresh parsley
- salt and pepper

Illustrated on page 66

The rather high fat content of the walnuts in this dish is offset by the high-fibre, low-calorie spaghetti.

PREPARATION TIME: 10 mins

COOKING TIME: 15 mins (plus 15 mins for the pasta)

SERVES 4

METHOD

1 Cook the spaghetti in 4 pints (2½ litres) of boiling water with a little lemon juice, for 12 minutes (3–4 minutes for fresh pasta).

2 Meanwhile, for the sauce, place the ground nuts in a small saucepan. Mix in the garlic, gradually add the milk, then add 2 tbsp (30ml) chopped parsley and season. Simmer for 10 minutes.

3 Drain the cooked spaghetti, mix with the sauce and serve.

FRESH HERB SPAGHETTI

INGREDIENTS

- 12oz (375g) wholemeal spaghetti
- 1 tsp (5ml) lemon juice
- 2 tbsp (30ml) olive oil
- 1 tbsp (15ml) lemon juice
- 3 tbsp (45ml) chopped fresh parsley
- 1 tbsp (15ml) chopped fresh mint
- 1oz (25g) grated Parmesan cheese

Illustrated on page 66

The herbs in this dish give the sauce a fresh, tangy flavour; here dried herbs will not achieve the same result. Always chop fresh herbs just before using them, otherwise their vitamin value will be lost.

PREPARATION TIME: 5 mins

COOKING TIME: 15 mins

SERVES 4

METHOD

1 Cook the spaghetti in 4 pints (2½ litres) of boiling water with a little lemon juice, for 12 minutes (3–4 minutes for fresh pasta).

2 Meanwhile, for the sauce, combine the olive oil and lemon juice. Add the chopped herbs and mix well.

3 Thoroughly drain the cooked spaghetti and return it to the pan. Pour over the herb sauce and mix well. Serve immediately, sprinkled with Parmesan cheese.

SPINACH AND CHEESE SPAGHETTI

INGREDIENTS

- 2lb (1kg) fresh spinach (or 1 lb/500g frozen chopped spinach)
- 2 tsp (10ml) arrowroot or cornflour
- 4oz (125g) skimmed milk soft cheese (quark)
- ½ pint (300ml) skimmed milk
- 2 tbsp (30ml) lemon juice
- ¼ tsp ground nutmeg
- salt and pepper
- 12oz (375g) wholemeal spaghetti
- 1 tsp (5ml) lemon juice
- 1oz (25g) grated Parmesan cheese

Illustrated below

Skimmed milk soft cheese (quark) reduces the fat content of this dish.

PREPARATION TIME: 15 mins
COOKING TIME: 15 mins (plus 12 mins for the pasta)
SERVES 4

METHOD

1 For the sauce, prepare the fresh spinach by washing the leaves and removing any tough stalks. Cook in a heavy-based saucepan, without adding extra liquid, for about 5 minutes until tender.

2 Put the cooked spinach, arrowroot or cornflour, cheese and skimmed milk in a blender or food processor, together with the lemon juice and the nutmeg. Blend until smooth and season to taste. Heat the spinach purée gently until it boils. Reduce the heat and simmer for 5 minutes.

3 Cook the spaghetti in 4 pints (2½ litres) of boiling water with a little lemon juice, for 12 minutes (3–4 minutes for fresh pasta).

4 When the spaghetti is cooked, drain well. Serve with the sauce spooned on top and sprinkled with the Parmesan cheese.

CLOCKWISE FROM TOP: Spaghetti with red lentil sauce; Spinach and cheese spaghetti; Wholewheat spaghetti with walnut and parsley sauce (see p.65); Fresh herb spaghetti (see p.65)

USING A PASTA MACHINE

*H*and-operated pasta machines have one set of plain rollers with variable width adjustments and one or more rollers for cutting shapes. Electric machines mix and knead the dough automatically before shaping.

1 *Take about 1oz (25g) of dough and roll it into a small sausage shape.*

2 *Set the plain rollers to their widest width and pass the dough through the rollers.*

3 *Reduce the roller width by one notch and re-roll the dough. Continue until the dough is thin enough.*

SPAGHETTI WITH RED LENTIL SAUCE

INGREDIENTS

- 6oz (175g) split red lentils
- 2 tsp (10ml) olive oil
- 1 onion, finely chopped
- 1 clove garlic, crushed
- ½ tsp ground allspice
- ¼ tsp celery seeds or 1 stick celery, finely chopped
- 14oz (400g) can of chopped tomatoes, with their juice
- 3 tbsp (45ml) red wine
- 1 tbsp (15ml) lemon juice
- 2 tsp (10ml) chopped fresh marjoram
- salt and pepper
- 12oz (375g) wholemeal spaghetti
- 1 tsp (5ml) lemon juice
- 1oz (25g) grated Parmesan cheese

Illustrated far left

Split red lentils need no soaking and cook very quickly. In this dish their mild flavour is enhanced by wine, herbs and spices.

PREPARATION TIME: 45 mins
COOKING TIME: 10 mins (plus 15 mins for the pasta)
SERVES 4

METHOD

1 For the sauce, place the lentils in a large saucepan with ¾ pint (450ml) water. Bring to the boil, then reduce the heat, cover and simmer for 30 minutes until the lentils have cooked into a purée.

2 Heat the olive oil and fry the onion and garlic for about 5 minutes until the onion is soft. Add the allspice, celery seeds or celery and lentils and cook gently for a further 5 minutes to allow the flavours to mingle.

3 Add the tomatoes to the lentil and onion mixture. Stir in the red wine, lemon juice and marjoram. Bring to the boil, reduce the heat and simmer for 10 minutes. Season to taste.

4 Meanwhile, cook the spaghetti in 4 pints (2½ litres) of boiling water with a little lemon juice, for 12 minutes (3–4 minutes for fresh pasta). Drain it well and serve with the sauce and Parmesan cheese.

WHOLEMEAL SPAGHETTI BAKE

INGREDIENTS

- 2 tsp (10ml) olive oil
- 1 onion, finely chopped
- 1 clove garlic, crushed
- 4oz (125g) mushrooms, sliced
- 1 eating apple, cored and grated
- 14oz (400g) can of chopped tomatoes
- 1 tsp (5ml) chopped fresh sage
- 2 tbsp (30ml) tomato purée
- 8oz (250g) wholemeal spaghetti
- 2oz (50g) Cheddar cheese, grated

Illustrated below

Wholemeal spaghetti contains more nutrients and fibre than ordinary pasta and combines with herbs and tomatoes to make a satisfying lunch or supper dish. If you wish to assemble the recipe in advance and bake it in the oven just before serving, add a little extra tomato juice to the sauce, as the consistency of the dish becomes thicker on standing.

PREPARATION TIME: 40 mins
COOKING TIME: 25 mins
SERVES 4

METHOD

1 Heat the oil in a large pan and gently fry the onion and garlic for 5 minutes.

2 Add the mushrooms, cover and cook for a further 5 minutes.

3 Stir in the apple. Drain the tomatoes, reserving the juice. Add the tomatoes to the pan with the sage and tomato purée. Cover and simmer gently for 10 minutes, adding a little tomato juice or water to make a thick sauce, if necessary.

4 Meanwhile, cook the spaghetti in a saucepan of boiling water for 5–7 minutes until it is just tender. Drain.

5 Mix the sauce and spaghetti together and put into a large casserole or ovenproof dish. Sprinkle over the cheese.

6 Bake in a preheated oven at Gas Mark 4, 350°F, 180°C for 20–25 minutes until golden brown and bubbling.

FROM TOP: Red lentil lasagne (see p.68); Wholemeal spaghetti bake

RED LENTIL LASAGNE

INGREDIENTS

- 2 tsp (10ml) olive oil
- 1 large onion, chopped
- 1 clove garlic, crushed
- 1 red or green pepper, deseeded and chopped
- 4oz (125g) mushrooms, thickly sliced
- 2 tsp (10ml) chopped fresh basil
- 2 tsp (10ml) chopped fresh oregano
- 8oz (250g) red split lentils
- 14oz (400g) can of chopped tomatoes
- 4½–5 pints (2½–3 litres) water
- 1 bay leaf
- salt and pepper
- 4oz (125g) wholemeal lasagne (approximately 8 sheets)
- 1oz (25g) margarine
- 1oz (25g) wholemeal flour
- ½ pint (300ml) skimmed milk
- ½ tsp mustard powder
- 3oz (75g) Cheddar cheese, grated

Illustrated on page 67

Various types of lasagne are available including stoneground, wholemeal and spinach-flavoured. If you use lasagne that does not need pre-cooking you will need to add extra liquid to the lentil sauce and cook according to the directions on the lasagne packet.

PREPARATION TIME: 1¼ hours
COOKING TIME: 35 mins
SERVES 4—6

METHOD

1 Heat the oil in a large pan and gently fry the onion and garlic over a moderate heat for 5 minutes. Add the pepper and mushrooms and cook for 5 minutes. Add the basil, oregano and lentils, and cook gently for 2–3 minutes. Stir in the tomatoes and their juice with ½ pint (300ml) of the water and the bay leaf.

2 Bring to the boil, cover, and simmer for 20–25 minutes until the lentils are soft. Add a little extra water if the mixture seems too dry. Season with salt and pepper, then remove the bay leaf.

3 Meanwhile, put the lasagne into a large saucepan of boiling water and simmer for 8–10 minutes until just tender. Drain, put into a bowl and cover with cold water.

4 Melt the margarine in a small pan and stir in the flour. Cook over a gentle heat for 3–4 minutes, stirring. Remove from the heat and gradually stir in the milk. Bring to the boil, stirring all the time, until the sauce thickens. Cook gently for 3–4 minutes, stirring. Remove from the heat and beat in the mustard powder and most of the cheese. Check the seasoning.

5 Put a third of the lentil mixture into the base of a deep casserole or ovenproof dish. Cover with a third of the lasagne, then add another third of the lentils, followed by another third of the lasagne. Cover this with half of the cheese sauce, then with the rest of the lentils. Top with the remaining lasagne. Pour the rest of the cheese sauce over the top and sprinkle with the cheese.

6 Bake in a preheated oven at Gas Mark 4, 350°F, 180°C for 30–35 minutes until bubbling and golden brown. Serve hot.

Wholemeal macaroni cheese with fennel

WHOLEMEAL MACARONI CHEESE WITH FENNEL

INGREDIENTS

- 6oz (175g) wholemeal macaroni
- ½ pint (300ml) skimmed milk
- ½ onion
- 1 bay leaf
- 1½oz (40g) margarine
- 1oz (25g) wholemeal flour
- 2 tbsp (30ml) chopped chives or spring onion tops
- ½ tsp black pepper
- ½ tsp yeast extract
- 1 head fennel, roughly chopped
- 2oz (50g) Cheddar cheese or low-fat hard cheese, grated
- salt and pepper

GARNISH

- fennel fronds

Illustrated left

This is a healthy version of the classic macaroni cheese, using wholemeal pasta, skimmed milk and only a little cheese, to keep the fat content down. Pasta and cheese together are a good source of protein. The addition of raw fennel towards the end of the cooking time gives a contrasting crunchy texture to the dish. Serve with a salad or green vegetables.

PREPARATION TIME: 40 mins

COOKING TIME: 25 mins

SERVES 4

METHOD

1 Cook the macaroni in a saucepan of boiling water for 7–10 minutes until just tender. Drain well.

2 Heat the milk, onion and bay leaf in a small saucepan. Bring to the boil, remove from the heat and allow the milk to infuse for 10 minutes.

3 Melt the margarine over a moderate heat in a small pan. Stir in the flour and cook gently for 3–4 minutes to form a soft roux.

4 Remove the onion and bay leaf from the milk. Gradually add the milk to the roux, stirring constantly. Bring to the boil over a moderate heat, stirring well as the sauce thickens.

5 Stir in the chives, black pepper, yeast extract, cooked macaroni and chopped fennel. Check the seasoning and cook for 2–3 minutes.

6 Transfer the mixture to a casserole or ovenproof dish and top with the grated cheese. Bake in a preheated oven at Gas Mark 5, 375°F, 190°C for 25 minutes until golden brown. Alternatively, cook under a preheated moderate grill for 10–15 minutes. Serve hot, garnished with the fronds of fennel.

FROM TOP: Macaroni in ginger and tomato sauce (see p.70); Spicy pepper macaroni; Vegetable tagliatelle with cheese and tomato sauce (see p.71)

SPICY PEPPER MACARONI

INGREDIENTS

- 12oz (375g) wholemeal macaroni
- 1 tsp (5ml) lemon juice
- 2 tsp (10ml) olive oil
- 1 dried red chilli pepper
- 1 clove garlic, crushed
- 2 red peppers, deseeded and chopped

GARNISH

- chopped fresh parsley

Illustrated above

This recipe is definitely for those who like their flavours hot!

PREPARATION TIME: 5 mins

COOKING TIME: 5 mins (plus 10 mins for the pasta)

SERVES 4

METHOD

1 Cook the macaroni by simmering in 4 pints (2½ litres) of water with a little lemon juice, for 10 minutes.

2 Meanwhile, heat the oil and fry the dried red chilli pepper for 2–3 minutes until blackened. Remove with a slotted spoon and discard.

3 Allow the oil to cool slightly. Add the garlic and red peppers. Cook over a medium heat for 5 minutes until the peppers are tender. Stir occasionally while they are cooking.

4 When the macaroni is cooked, drain well. Mix with the peppers and garnish.

MACARONI IN GINGER AND TOMATO SAUCE

INGREDIENTS

- 2 tsp (10ml) olive oil
- 1 onion, finely chopped
- 4 celery sticks, trimmed and finely chopped
- 2 tbsp (30ml) finely chopped fresh root ginger
- 1½lb (800g) can of peeled tomatoes
- 2 tsp (10ml) chopped marjoram
- 3 tbsp (45ml) tomato purée
- 12oz (375g) wholemeal macaroni
- 1 tsp (5ml) lemon juice
- salt and pepper

GARNISH

- 1oz (25g) grated Parmesan cheese
- 1 tsp (5ml) chopped fresh parsley

Illustrated on page 69

Canned tomatoes tend to have a stronger colour and flavour than most of the fresh ones which are readily available. However, if you are going to use fresh tomatoes then you will need about 2lb (1kg), peeled and chopped.

PREPARATION TIME: 10 minutes
COOKING TIME: 15 mins (plus 10 mins for the pasta)
SERVES 4

METHOD

1 For the sauce, heat the oil in a medium-sized saucepan and gently fry the onion and celery in the oil for 5 minutes until soft. Add the ginger and cook gently for a further 2 minutes to allow the flavours to mingle.
2 Add the tomatoes, marjoram and tomato purée. Bring to the boil. Reduce the heat and simmer for 15 minutes until the tomatoes are cooked.
3 Meanwhile, cook the macaroni by simmering in 4 pints (2½ litres) of water with a little lemon juice for 10 minutes.
4 When the macaroni is cooked, drain well. Mix with the sauce, season and serve garnished with Parmesan and chopped parsley.

MAKING TAGLIATELLE

*T*agliatelle is the Italian name for noodles; long ribbon-like strips of pasta. It is very similar to fettucine. You can also get green tagliatelle (known as tagliatelle verde) which is flavoured with spinach. Tagliatelle is delicious served with simple sauces which are quick and easy to make, as well as more complicated ones. Combined with dairy products or pulses, it provides a rich protein.

1 *Make the pasta dough (see p.65). Leave to rest for 30 minutes. On a lightly floured surface, roll out a quarter of the dough into a rectangular shape, as thinly as possible.*

2 *Carefully roll up the dough like a Swiss roll. Cut through the roll with a sharp knife at ¼ inch (5mm) intervals.*

3 *Unroll each strip like a ribbon and lay out flat to dry.*

VEGETABLE TAGLIATELLE WITH CHEESE AND TOMATO SAUCE

INGREDIENTS

- 12oz (375g) wholemeal tagliatelle or ½ quantity of pasta dough see p.64
- 1 tsp (5ml) lemon juice
- 8oz (250g) green beans, topped and tailed
- 8oz (250g) carrots, cut into strips
- 8oz (250g) tomatoes, skinned
- 2oz (50g) skimmed milk soft cheese (quark)
- salt and pepper

Illustrated on page 69

This combination of vegetables with skimmed milk soft cheese keeps the vitamin content high and the fat content very low.

PREPARATION TIME: 10 mins (plus 40 mins for the pasta)

COOKING TIME: 10 mins

SERVES 4

METHOD

1 If using home-made tagliatelle, see p.70. Then cook the tagliatelle by simmering in 4 pints (2½ litres) of water with a little lemon juice, for 4 minutes (8 minutes for dried pasta).
2 Meanwhile, for the sauce, steam the beans and carrots for 5 minutes until tender.
3 Put the tomatoes and cheese into a blender or food processor and purée until smooth. Season to taste.
4 Drain the tagliatelle well. Mix with the beans and carrots and the cheese and tomato sauce. Reheat and serve.

LASAGNE WITH BEAN AND TOMATO SAUCE

INGREDIENTS

- 8oz (250g) haricot or black-eyed beans, soaked
- 2 tsp (10ml) olive oil
- 1 onion, finely chopped
- 2 cloves garlic, crushed
- 1 tsp (5ml) cumin seeds
- 12oz (375g) tomatoes, chopped
- 2 tbsp (30ml) tomato purée
- 1 tbsp (15ml) soya sauce
- salt and pepper
- 6oz (175g) wholemeal lasagne
- 1 tsp (5ml) lemon juice
- ½ pint (300ml) natural yogurt
- 1 tsp (5ml) arrowroot or cornflour

Illustrated left

Dried beans, or pulses, are an excellent source of fibre and protein.

PREPARATION TIME: 30 mins (plus 10–12 hours soaking time and 40 mins for the pasta)

COOKING TIME: 40 mins (plus 50 mins for the beans and 20 mins for the pasta)

SERVES 4

METHOD

1 For the sauce, place the soaked beans into a large saucepan and cover with fresh water. Bring to the boil. Boil fast for 10 minutes, then reduce the heat and simmer for a further 35–40 minutes until the beans are cooked. Drain the beans, reserving ½ pint (300ml) of the cooking liquid.
2 Heat the oil in a medium-sized saucepan and gently fry the onion and garlic for 5 minutes until the onion is soft but not browned. Add the cumin, beans and tomatoes and cook for 5 minutes.
3 Add the ½ pint (300ml) reserved cooking liquid, tomato purée, soya sauce and seasoning. Bring to the boil. Reduce the heat and simmer for 10 minutes.
4 Meanwhile, cook the lasagne by simmering in 4 pints (2½ litres) of water with a little lemon juice, for 16 minutes (4 minutes for fresh pasta). Keep in a bowl of cold water until ready to use.
5 For the topping, mix 1 tbsp (15ml) yogurt with the arrowroot or cornflour in a small pan to give a smooth paste. Add the rest of the yogurt and stir in. Bring to the boil over a moderate heat.
6 Grease a 3-pint (1.8-litre) ovenproof dish. Spread about 4 tbsp (60ml) bean sauce over the bottom of the dish. Then layer alternately with lasagne, half the remaining bean sauce, lasagne, the rest of the bean sauce and, finally, the rest of the lasagne. Cover with the yogurt topping.
7 Bake in a preheated oven at Gas Mark 6, 400°F, 200°C for 40 minutes until browned on top.

FROM LEFT: Lasagne with bean and tomato sauce; Aubergine, pepper and mushroom lasagne (see p.72)

AUBERGINE, PEPPER AND MUSHROOM LASAGNE

INGREDIENTS

- 2 tbsp (30ml) olive oil
- 1 onion, finely chopped
- 1 clove garlic, crushed
- 1 red pepper, deseeded and diced
- 1 green pepper, deseeded and diced
- 8oz (250g) button mushrooms, sliced
- 1 lb (500g) aubergine, cut into ½ inch (1cm) cubes
- ½ pint (300ml) vegetable stock or water
- 4 tsp (20ml) chopped fresh oregano
- 4 tbsp (60ml) chopped fresh parsley
- 1½oz (40g) margarine or butter
- 1oz (25g) wholemeal flour
- ½ tsp mustard powder
- ¾ pint (450ml) skimmed milk
- 6oz (175g) dried wholemeal lasagne (the type that does not require pre-cooking)
- 1oz (25g) Cheddar cheese, grated

Illustrated on page 71

The sauce for the filling needs to be more liquid than normal with this lasagne as it is not pre-cooked.

PREPARATION TIME: 50 mins
COOKING TIME: 45 mins
SERVES 4

METHOD

1 For the vegetable sauce, heat the oil and fry the onion, garlic, red and green pepper for about 5 minutes. Add the mushrooms and aubergine. Cover and cook over a low heat for 10 minutes, stirring occasionally. Add the stock, oregano and parsley. Boil, then reduce the heat, cover and cook for 10 minutes.
2 For the white sauce, melt the margarine in a small pan. Add the flour. Cook over a medium heat, stirring constantly for 3 minutes. Add the mustard powder. Gradually add the milk and boil, stirring constantly. Reduce the heat and simmer until the sauce thickens.
3 Grease a 3-pint (1.8-litre) ovenproof dish. Spread about 4 tbsp (60ml) white sauce over the bottom of the dish. Then layer the dish alternately with lasagne, half the aubergine sauce, another layer of lasagne, the remaining aubergine sauce and, finally, the rest of the lasagne. Cover with the remaining white sauce and sprinkle the grated cheese on top.
4 Bake in a preheated oven at Gas Mark 6, 400°F, 200°C for 45 minutes until bubbling and golden brown on top.

MAKING RAVIOLI

*R*avioli is a term referring to all the basic pocket-shaped pastas. These are usually small, square parcels, stuffed and served with a sauce. If the ravioli is not going to be cooked straight away, leave it to dry on a lightly floured surface.

1 Roll out a quarter of the dough into a large oblong. Mark a grid pattern of 1 inch (2.5cm) squares on one half.

2 Put small spoonfuls of the filling mixture in the centre of each marked-out square. Moisten round the edges.

3 Fold over the plain half. Press down well between each mound and then cut between them with a serrated pastry wheel.

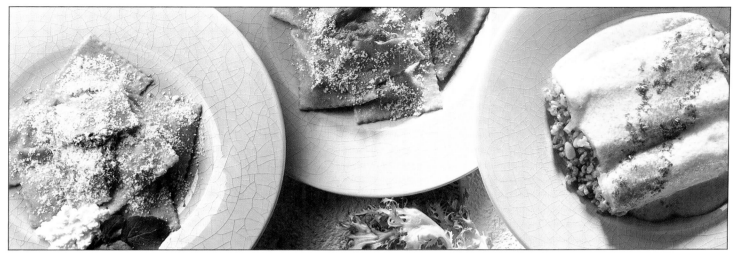

FROM LEFT: Spinach and cottage cheese ravioli (see p.74); Olive and tomato ravioli; Rice and egg cannelloni

OLIVE AND TOMATO RAVIOLI

INGREDIENTS

■ ½ quantity of pasta dough (see p.64)
■ 2 tsp (10ml) olive oil
■ 1 onion, finely chopped
■ ½ tsp ground cumin
■ 3 tbsp (45ml) tomato purée
■ 3oz (75g) black olives, stoned and chopped

GARNISH

■ 1oz (25g) grated Parmesan cheese

Illustrated above

This combination of olives, tomato and onion is classically Italian.

PREPARATION TIME: 30 mins (plus 40 mins for the pasta)
COOKING TIME: 8 mins
SERVES 4

METHOD

1 Make the ravioli dough (see p.64). For the filling, heat the oil and fry the onion for 5 minutes, add the cumin, tomato purée and olives and cook for 5 minutes more. Season and cool.
2 Take half of the dough and roll into a large oblong. Mark a grid of 1 inch (2.5cm) squares on one half. Put half of the filling in the centre of each square, and moisten the edges of each square. Fold the plain half over the filling and cut into squares (see p.72). Repeat with the remaining dough. If the ravioli is not going to be cooked straightaway, leave to dry on a floured surface.
3 Cook the ravioli a few at a time by simmering in water for 8 minutes. Garnish with Parmesan.

RICE AND EGG CANNELLONI

INGREDIENTS

■ 6oz (175g) cannelloni (about 16 tubes) or ¼ quantity of pasta dough (see p.64)
■ 2 tsp (10ml) olive oil
■ 1 onion, finely chopped
■ 12oz (375g) brown rice
■ 2 hard-boiled eggs, chopped
■ 2oz (50g) pine kernels or chopped almonds
■ 2 tbsp (30ml) chopped parsley
■ 2 tsp (10ml) paprika
■ 1½oz (40g) margarine or butter
■ 1oz (25g) wholemeal flour
■ 2 tsp (10ml) mustard powder
■ 1 pint (600ml) skimmed milk

Illustrated above

Measure the rice water accurately so none of the nutrients are lost.

PREPARATION TIME: 45 mins (plus 40 mins for the pasta)
COOKING TIME: 40 mins
SERVES 4

METHOD

1 For home-made cannelloni, see p.74.
2 For the stuffing, heat the oil and fry the onion for 5 minutes. Add the rice and cook for 5 minutes. Add 1 pint 2 fl oz (650ml) of hot water, boil, then cover and simmer for 25 minutes. Remove from the heat. Add the eggs, pine kernels or almonds, parsley and paprika.
3 For the sauce, melt the margarine, add the flour and cook for 3 minutes. Stir in the mustard. Gradually add the milk. Simmer for 5 minutes.
4 Add a quarter of the sauce to the rice mixture and stir in well.
5 Fill the cannelloni with the stuffing, transfer to a greased ovenproof dish, and pour on the remaining sauce. Bake in a preheated oven at Gas Mark 5, 375°F, 190°C for 40 minutes.

SPINACH AND COTTAGE CHEESE RAVIOLI

INGREDIENTS

- ½ quantity of pasta dough (see p. 64)
- 8oz (250g) fresh spinach
- 3oz (75g) cottage cheese
- ¼ tsp ground nutmeg
- 1 tsp (5ml) lemon juice

GARNISH

- 1oz (25g) grated Parmesan cheese

Illustrated on page 73

It is very important not to overcook the spinach as this would destroy most of the nutrients.

PREPARATION TIME: 30 mins (plus 40 mins for the pasta)

COOKING TIME: 8 mins

SERVES 4

METHOD

1 Make the ravioli dough (see p.64).
2 For the filling, wash the spinach, removing any tough stalks. Put into a heavy-based saucepan without extra liquid. Cook over a medium heat for 5 minutes, stirring occasionally. Chop finely. Mix with the cottage cheese and nutmeg.
3 Take half of the pasta dough and roll into a large oblong. Mark a grid pattern of 1-inch (2.5cm) squares on one half (see p.72).
4 Put half of the filling, in small spoonfuls, in the centre of each square. Moisten the edges of each square with water. Fold the plain half of the oblong over the filling. Press down well between each mound. Cut into squares. Repeat with the remaining dough.
5 If the ravioli is not going to be cooked straightaway leave to dry.
6 Cook the ravioli by simmering, a few at a time, in 4 pints (2½ litres) of water with a little lemon juice, for 8 minutes. Garnish with Parmesan and serve immediately.

MAKING CANNELLONI

*C*annelloni is the Italian name for large squares of pasta which have been rolled into tubes and served with a stuffing and sauce. They can be made as sweet or savoury dishes and are quite substantial.

1 Make the dough (see p. 65). Leave to rest for 30 minutes. Roll out a quarter of the dough very thinly.

2 Cut into rectangles measuring 4 × 3 inches (10 × 7cm).

3 Put about 2 tbsp (30ml) of filling on each rectangle. Moisten the edges, roll up into a tube shape and cook.

BASIC PIZZA DOUGH

INGREDIENTS

- 1oz (25g) fresh yeast (or 2 tsp/10ml dried yeast)
- ½ pint (300ml) lukewarm water
- 1lb (500g) wholemeal flour
- 1oz (25g) soya flour (optional)

This dough is sufficient for four bases, each of which makes a pizza for 4.
MAKES ABOUT: 1lb 10oz/800g of dough, or 4 × 7oz/200g pizzas

METHOD

1 Mix the fresh yeast with the lukewarm water (see p.76).
2 Combine the flours and pour over the yeast mixture. Mix well and turn out. Knead for 5–10 minutes until smooth and elastic.
3 Transfer into a clean bowl and cover with clingfilm or a damp cloth. Leave to rise for about 30 minutes.

NEAPOLITAN PIZZA

INGREDIENTS

- ¼ quantity of pizza dough (see above)
- 2 tsp (10ml) olive oil
- 2 large onions, finely chopped
- 1 clove garlic, crushed
- 14oz (400g) can of chopped tomatoes
- 4 tsp (20ml) chopped fresh oregano
- 1 bay leaf
- 2 tbsp (30ml) tomato purée
- 1 onion, sliced into fine rings
- 3 tomatoes, sliced

Illustrated right

The classic Italian combination of tomatoes and oregano works beautifully in this, the most basic of all pizzas.
PREPARATION TIME: 40 mins (plus 50 mins for the dough)
COOKING TIME: 25 mins
SERVES 4

METHOD

1 Make the pizza dough and leave to rise. Meanwhile, make the sauce. Fry the onions and garlic for 5 minutes, add the tomatoes, oregano, bay leaf and tomato purée. Boil, then simmer for 20 minutes, stirring occasionally. Remove from the heat and leave to cool. Discard the bay leaf. Season to taste.
2 Knead the dough lightly. Roll out to fit a greased 10 inch (25cm) round baking tray.
3 Spread the sauce over the base. Garnish with the onion and tomato. Brush the onion and tomato with oil to prevent drying. Bake for 25 minutes. Serve immediately.

FROM LEFT: Pizza with onion topping (see p.76); Pizza with spinach purée; Neapolitan pizza

PIZZA WITH SPINACH PUREE

INGREDIENTS

- ¼ quantity of pizza dough (see above)
- 2lb (1kg) fresh spinach (or 10oz/300g frozen spinach)
- 2 tsp (10ml) olive oil
- 2 cloves garlic, crushed
- ¼ tsp ground nutmeg
- 4oz (125g) shelled peas, fresh or frozen
- 1 red pepper, deseeded and chopped
- 3 spring onions, sliced into rings
- 1oz (25g) grated Parmesan cheese

Illustrated above

The combination of spinach and peas makes a low-fat, high-protein pizza.
PREPARATION TIME: 35 mins (plus 50 mins for the dough)
COOKING TIME: 20 mins
SERVES 4

METHOD

1 Make the pizza dough and leave to rise. For the sauce, wash the fresh spinach and remove the tougher stalks. Fry the garlic for 2 minutes, add the spinach and cook for 5 minutes (cook frozen spinach according to instructions). Add the nutmeg and purée. Steam the peas for 5 minutes.
2 Knead the dough lightly, then roll out to fit a greased 10-inch (25cm) round baking tray.
3 Spread the purée over the dough. Garnish with peas, pepper and spring onions, and sprinkle with Parmesan. Bake in a preheated oven at Gas Mark 6, 400°F, 200°C for 20 minutes.

MAKING PIZZA BASES

*Y*ou can, if you like, bake pizzas without any topping (at Gas Mark 6, 400°F, 200°C for 8 minutes). Either shape the dough into a round by passing from hand to hand to flatten it, or use a rolling pin to roll out the dough on a lightly floured surface.

1 Mix the yeast and water. Add the flour and mix well.

2 Knead for 5–10 minutes, then leave to rise for 30 minutes.

3 Roll out the dough to give a 10-inch (25cm) round.

PIZZA WITH ONION TOPPING

INGREDIENTS

- ¼ quantity of pizza dough (see p.75)
- 2 tsp (10ml) olive oil
- 1lb (500g) onions, finely chopped
- 1 clove garlic, crushed
- 2 tbsp (30ml) tomato purée
- 2 tsp (10ml) chopped fresh marjoram
- 8oz (250g) potatoes, thinly sliced
- 2 tsp (10ml) olive oil
- 1 tbsp (15ml) lemon juice
- 1oz (25g) slivered almonds

Illustrated on page 75

The onions provide the main flavour in this pizza sauce. Sprinkling them with salt is one way to bring out their juices even more, but a much healthier alternative is to cook them on a low heat, stirring occasionally so that they do not brown.

PREPARATION TIME: 35 mins (plus 50 mins for the dough)
COOKING TIME: 30 mins
SERVES 4

METHOD

1 Make the pizza dough and leave to rise. Make the sauce by heating the oil in a medium-sized saucepan. Gently fry the onions and garlic for 5 minutes until the onions are soft but not browned. Reduce the heat and simmer for a further 10 minutes, stirring occasionally, until the onions are tender and juicy.
2 Remove from the heat. Add the tomato purée and marjoram and mix well. Season to taste and allow to cool.
3 Grease a 10-inch (25cm) baking tray. Knock back the dough by kneading lightly. Roll out to a 10-inch (25cm) round on a slightly floured surface and put into the baking tray.
4 Spread the topping evenly over the base. Garnish with the sliced potatoes. Mix together the olive oil and lemon juice and brush over the potatoes.
5 Bake in a preheated oven at Gas Mark 6, 400°F, 200°C for 25 minutes, until the potatoes and the base are cooked through.
6 Remove from the oven. Sprinkle over the slivered almonds and return to the oven for 5 minutes until the almonds are beginning to brown.

HARICOT BEAN AND PEPPER PIZZA

INGREDIENTS

- ¼ quantity of pizza dough (see p.75)
- 8oz (250g) haricot beans, soaked
- 2 tsp (10ml) olive oil
- 12oz (375g) onions, finely chopped
- 2 cloves garlic, crushed
- 2 tbsp (30ml) lemon juice
- 2 tsp (10ml) chopped fresh tarragon
- salt and pepper
- yellow pepper
- 12 green olives, stuffed with pimento

Illustrated below

Haricot beans with onions make a highly nutritious pizza topping.
PREPARATION TIME: 30 mins (plus 10–12 hours soaking time and 50 mins for the dough)
COOKING TIME: 25 mins (plus 50 mins for the beans)
SERVES 4

METHOD

1 Make the pizza dough and leave to rise. Boil the beans fast for 10 minutes in fresh water. Simmer for 40 minutes and drain.
2 Heat the oil and fry the onion and garlic for 5 minutes. Add the beans, lemon juice and tarragon. Cook gently for a further 5 minutes, stirring occasionally, then season and purée.
3 Grease a 10-inch (25cm) baking tray. Knock back the dough by kneading lightly. Roll out to a 10-inch (25cm) round on a lightly floured surface and put on the baking tray.
4 Spread the bean purée over the dough. Garnish with the pepper rings and olives. Bake in a preheated oven at Gas Mark 6, 400°F, 200°C for 25 minutes.

TOMATO AND CHILLI PIZZA

INGREDIENTS

- ¼ quantity of pizza dough (see p.75)
- 2 tsp (10ml) olive oil
- 1 dried red chilli pepper
- 1 onion, finely chopped
- 1 clove garlic, crushed
- 14oz (400g) can of chopped tomatoes
- 1 tbsp (15ml) tomato purée
- 1 tsp (5ml) fresh green peppercorns
- ½ a yellow, a green and a red pepper, deseeded and cut into strips

Illustrated left

The chilli pepper and green peppercorns give this pizza a spicy flavour.
PREPARATION TIME: 45 mins (plus 50 mins for the dough)
COOKING TIME: 25 mins
SERVES 4

METHOD

1 Make the pizza dough and leave to rise. For the sauce heat the oil and fry the chilli pepper for 3 minutes, press gently with a slotted spoon, then discard. Allow the oil to cool, add the onion and garlic and fry for 5 minutes. Add the tomatoes, purée and peppercorns. Simmer for 20 minutes.
2 Roll out the dough to fit a greased 11 × 7-inch (28 × 18cm) Swiss roll tin. Spread with the sauce and decorate with the peppers. Bake in a preheated oven at Gas Mark 6, 400°F, 200°C for 25 minutes.

MOZZARELLA AND TOMATO PIZZA

INGREDIENTS

- ¼ quantity of pizza dough (see p.75)
- 2 tsp (10ml) olive oil
- 1 onion, finely chopped
- 1 clove garlic, crushed
- 14oz (400g) can of chopped tomatoes
- 1 tbsp (15ml) tomato purée
- 2 tsp (10ml) chopped fresh basil
- salt and pepper
- 1oz (25g) pine kernels or sunflower seeds
- 12 black olives, stoned
- 1oz (25g) sultanas
- 2 tsp (10ml) capers
- 2oz (50g) sliced Mozzarella cheese

Illustrated left

Mozzarella cheese is rather high in fat, but just a little can be made to go a long way.
PREPARATION TIME: 40 mins (plus 50 mins for making the dough)
COOKING TIME: 25 mins
SERVES 4

METHOD

1 Make the pizza dough and leave to rise. Meanwhile, to make the sauce, heat the oil and fry the onion and garlic for 5 minutes. Add the tomatoes, tomato purée and basil. Bring to the boil, then simmer for 20 minutes. Season to taste and allow to cool.
2 Grease a 10-inch (25cm) round baking tray. Lightly knead the dough and roll out to fit the tray.
3 Spread the tomato sauce over the dough. Garnish with the pine kernels or sunflower seeds, olives, sultanas, capers and Mozzarella. Bake in a preheated oven at Gas Mark 6, 400°F, 200°C for 25 minutes until the cheese is bubbling.

FROM LEFT: Haricot bean and pepper pizza; Tomato and chilli pizza; Mozzarella and tomato pizza

FROM LEFT: Cheese and leek pizza; Pizza pockets with broad beans

■ CHEESE AND LEEK PIZZA ■

INGREDIENTS

■ ¼ quantity of pizza dough (see p.75)
■ 1lb (500g) carrots, sliced
■ ½oz (15g) sunflower seeds
■ 2 tsp (10ml) sunflower oil
■ 1lb (500g) leeks, sliced
■ 1 tbsp (15ml) grated fresh root ginger
■ 1 tbsp (15ml) chopped fresh parsley
■ 1oz (25g) raisins
■ 1oz (25g grated Parmesan cheese

Illustrated above

Carrots and leeks make an unusual combination in this pizza sauce.
PREPARATION TIME: 45 mins (plus 50 mins for the dough)
COOKING TIME: 25 mins
SERVES 4

METHOD

1 Make the pizza dough and leave to rise. Meanwhile, for the sauce, steam the carrots for 10 minutes, then purée. Toast the sunflower seeds in the oil for 5 minutes. Reduce the heat and add the leeks and ginger. Cook gently for 10 minutes.
2 Grease a 10-inch (25cm) round baking tray. Lightly knead the dough, then roll out to fit the tray.
3 Spread with the purée. Top with the leek and sunflower mixture and garnish with parsley, raisins and Parmesan. Bake in a preheated oven at Gas Mark 6, 400°F, 200°C for 25 minutes.

PIZZA POCKETS WITH BROAD BEANS ■

INGREDIENTS

■ ½ quantity of pizza dough (see p.75)
■ 2 tsp (10ml) olive oil
■ 1 onion, finely chopped
■ 1 clove garlic, crushed
■ 14oz (400g) can of chopped tomatoes
■ 1 tbsp (15ml) tomato purée
■ 2 tsp (10ml) chopped fresh oregano
■ 4oz (125g) broad beans
■ 2oz (50g) grated cheese

Illustrated above

These are delicious folded pizzas containing a filling.
PREPARATION TIME: 45 mins (plus 50 mins for the dough)
COOKING TIME: 25 mins
SERVES 4

METHOD

1 Make the dough and leave to rise. Heat the oil and fry the onion and garlic for 5 minutes. Add the tomatoes, purée and oregano. Boil, add the beans, then simmer for 20 minutes. Cool.
2 Roll the dough into four circular portions about 7 inches (18cm) in diameter. Spoon a quarter of the filling on to each circle. Moisten the edges with water, fold in half and seal. Sprinkle ½oz (15g) of grated cheese on each pizza. Place on a greased baking sheet. Bake in a preheated oven at Gas Mark 6, 400°F, 200°C for 25 minutes.

ROLLED PIZZA WITH A NUTTY TOMATO FILLING

INGREDIENTS

- ½ quantity of pizza dough (see p.75)
- 2 tsp (10ml) olive oil
- 1lb (500g) onions, finely chopped
- 2 cloves garlic, crushed
- 14oz (400g) can of chopped tomatoes
- 2 tbsp (30ml) tomato purée
- 2 tsp (10ml) allspice
- 4 tsp (20ml) finely chopped fresh basil
- 2oz (50g) coarsely chopped walnuts
- 2oz (50g) coarsely chopped almonds
- 4oz (125g) black olives, stoned and chopped
- 1oz (25g) Cheddar cheese, grated

Illustrated right

Walnuts and almonds give an unusual and interesting texture to pizza sauces and fillings, but while they are an excellent source of protein, they are also quite high in fat, and should therefore be used sparingly.

PREPARATION TIME: 20 mins (plus 50 mins for the dough)

COOKING TIME: 25 mins

SERVES 4

METHOD

1 Make the dough and leave to rest. Meanwhile, for the sauce, heat the oil and fry the onion and garlic for 5 minutes. Add the tomatoes, tomato purée, allspice, basil, walnuts, almonds and olives. Bring to the boil. Simmer for 20 minutes until the tomatoes are cooked.
2 Knock back the dough by kneading. Divide the dough in half. Roll out half on a lightly floured surface to give a rectangle measuring 11 × 7 inches (28 × 18cm). Put the dough on floured greaseproof paper or a tea towel.
3 Spread half of the tomato and nut sauce evenly over the dough. With the help of the greaseproof paper or tea towel, roll the pizza up along the longest edge so that it looks like a long Swiss roll. Transfer to a greased baking sheet. Repeat the rolling out and filling process with the other half of the dough.
4 Make diagonal cuts along the top of the rolls. Sprinkle with the grated cheese. Bake in a preheated oven at Gas Mark 6, 400°F, 200°C for 25 minutes until the base is cooked and the cheese has melted. Slice to serve.

PASTRY-BASE PIZZA WITH ROSEMARY SAUCE

INGREDIENTS

- 4oz (125g) wholemeal flour
- ½ tsp baking powder
- 1oz (25g) solid vegetable oil
- 1oz (25g) butter or margarine
- 2 tsp (10ml) sunflower oil
- 2 tsp (10ml) olive oil
- 1 onion, finely chopped
- 1 clove garlic, crushed
- 14oz (400g) can of chopped tomatoes
- 1 tbsp (15ml) tomato purée
- 1 tsp (5ml) chopped fresh rosemary
- 4oz (125g) button mushrooms, sliced
- 8 black and 8 green olives, stoned
- Parmesan cheese, grated

Illustrated below

Shortcrust pastry is higher in fat than yeasted pastry, so roll it thinly.

PREPARATION TIME: 40 mins (plus 40 mins for the dough)

COOKING TIME: 25 mins

SERVES 4

METHOD

1 For the base, mix the flour and baking powder and rub in the solid oil and butter until the mixture resembles fine breadcrumbs. Mix together the sunflower oil and 2–3 tbsp (30–45ml) water and sprinkle over the flour mixture. Mix to form a wet dough. Cover with clingfilm and refrigerate for 30 minutes.
2 Meanwhile, for the sauce, fry the onion and garlic. Add the tomatoes, purée and rosemary. Simmer for 20 minutes.
3 Roll out the pastry to fit a 10-inch (25cm) baking tray. Put on the tray and prick over with a fork. Bake in a preheated oven, Gas Mark 6, 400°F, 200°C for 10 minutes. Spread the sauce over the pastry. Garnish with mushrooms and olives and sprinkle with Parmesan. Return to the oven for 25 minutes. Serve hot or cold.

FROM LEFT: Rolled pizza with a nutty tomato filling; Pastry-base pizza with rosemary sauce

WHOLEMEAL PANCAKE BATTER

INGREDIENTS

- 1 egg
- ½ pint (300ml) skimmed milk
- 1 tsp (5ml) sunflower oil
- 4oz (125g) wholemeal flour

PREPARATION TIME: 5 mins (plus 30 mins resting time)
COOKING TIME: 30 mins
MAKES 8–10 pancakes

METHOD

1 Liquidize the egg, milk and oil in a blender or food processor for 30 seconds. Add the flour and liquidize for 30 seconds.
2 Heat a 7-inch (18cm) pancake pan. Put in a little oil and wipe over with absorbent kitchen paper. Pour in 2 tbsp (30ml) batter and cook for 2 minutes until the top has set. Loosen the edges of the pancake with a spatula. Cook the other side for 1 minute.

FROM LEFT: Artichoke and hazelnut pancakes; Aubergine pancakes

MAKING PANCAKES

A good pancake pan should be about 7 inches (18cm) in diameter across the base and have curved sides, so that the pancakes can be easily turned over and removed from the pan.

1 *Mix together the flour, egg, milk and oil in a mixing bowl. Beat well.*

2 *Pour a little batter into a hot pan and tilt so that the batter coats the bottom.*

3 *Cook for 2 minutes and then loosen the edge, toss and cook the other side.*

AUBERGINE PANCAKES

INGREDIENTS

- 1lb (500g) aubergines
- 1 quantity of wholemeal batter (see p.80)
- 2 tsp (10ml) olive oil
- 1 onion, chopped
- 4 cloves, garlic, crushed
- juice of 1 lemon
- ¼ tsp chilli powder
- 1 tbsp soya sauce
- 6 tbsp (90ml) chopped parsley
- ¼ pint (150ml) natural yogurt

GARNISH
- 1 tbsp (15ml) chopped parsley

Illustrated far left

Baking rather than frying the aubergines keeps this dish low in fat.
PREPARATION TIME: 45 mins plus (30 mins for the batter)
COOKING TIME: 15 mins (plus 30 mins for the pancakes)
MAKES: 8–10 pancakes

METHOD

1 For the filling, bake the aubergines in a preheated oven at Gas Mark 4, 350°F, 180°C for 30 minutes. Meanwhile, make the pancakes.
2 For the filling, fry the onion and garlic for 5 minutes. Skin the aubergine, then purée with the onion and garlic, lemon juice, chilli powder, soya sauce, parsley and 6 tbsp (90ml) yogurt.
3 Put 2 tbsp (30ml) of filling on each pancake and fold up. Arrange on an ovenproof dish and cover with foil. Heat through in the oven for 15 minutes. Serve with yogurt and parsley to garnish.

ARTICHOKE AND HAZELNUT PANCAKES

INGREDIENTS

- 1 quantity of wholemeal batter (see p.80)
- 2 tsp (10ml) sunflower oil
- 1 onion, finely chopped
- ½oz (15g) wholemeal flour
- ¼ pint (150ml) skimmed milk
- 4 artichoke hearts, fresh or canned
- 2oz (50g) hazelnuts
- ½ tsp chopped dill
- 1 tbsp (15ml) lemon juice
- 1oz (25g) grated Parmesan cheese

Illustrated far left

Artichoke hearts are delicious, but fiddly; canned ones are simpler.
PREPARATION TIME: 55 mins
COOKING TIME: 15 mins
MAKES: 8–10 pancakes

METHOD

1 Make the pancakes (see p.80). Then fry the onion. Add the flour and cook for 3 minutes, stirring. Gradually add the milk and boil, stirring. Reduce the heat.
2 Cut the artichoke hearts into quarters. Add to the sauce with the dill, chopped hazelnuts and lemon juice. Season and reheat.
3 Put 2 tbsp (30ml) of filling on each pancake and fold up. Put in an ovenproof dish, and sprinkle with Parmesan. Heat in a preheated oven, Gas Mark 4, 350°F, 180°C for 15 minutes.

Spiced pancakes

SPICED PANCAKES

INGREDIENTS

BATTER
- 1½oz (40g) wholemeal flour
- ¼ pint (150ml) semi-skimmed milk
- 1 small egg, size 6, beaten
- 1 tsp (5ml oil)

FILLING
- 6oz (175g) fennel or celery, chopped
- 6oz (175g) leeks, chopped
- 2oz (50g) curd cheese
- 4 fl oz (125ml) soured cream or smetana
- 6 cardamom seeds
- ½ tsp coriander seeds

Illustrated above

These thin, light pancakes have a low-fat, creamy filling flavoured with unusual curry spices.
PREPARATION TIME: 30 mins (plus 2 hours' standing time for the batter)
COOKING TIME: 8 mins
SERVES 4

METHOD

1 For the batter, mix all the ingredients together in a blender or food processor to form a thick, smooth mixture. Leave to stand for 1–2 hours.
2 For the filling, steam the fennel or celery and leeks for 6–10 minutes until tender. Whisk the curd cheese and soured cream or smetana until airy. Toast the seeds in a dry frying pan, crush them and fold into the soured cream mixture, then add the steamed vegetables.
3 Make 4 thin pancakes and set them aside. When cooked, fold them in half and then fold over so that they form a cornet. Fill and garnish with flaked almonds.

WHOLEMEAL PANCAKES WITH A SPICY BEAN FILLING

INGREDIENTS

- 12oz (375g) French beans, trimmed and diced
- 2 tsp (10ml) sunflower oil
- 1 onion, peeled and finely chopped
- 2 tsp (10ml) garam masala
- ½ tsp turmeric
- pinch chilli powder
- 14oz (400g) can chopped tomatoes
- ¼ pint (150ml) natural yogurt
- 1 tsp (5ml) cornflour
- salt and pepper

PANCAKES
- ½ pint (300ml) skimmed milk
- 1 egg
- 1 tsp (5ml) sunflower oil
- 4oz (125g) wholemeal flour
- pinch salt
- oil for frying

TO SERVE
- natural yogurt

Illustrated right

A pancake batter made with wholemeal flour and skimmed milk is not only lower in calories and fats than a traditional batter mixture, but also provides fibre, protein, and a large number of valuable minerals and vitamins. This spicy bean sauce would also combine well with grain dishes or nut roasts. You may find that the sauce curdles when you add the yogurt. If so, beat it well over a high heat and, although the appearance may change, the flavour will still be excellent.

PREPARATION TIME: 25 mins
COOKING TIME: 1 hour
SERVES 4

METHOD

1 Steam the French beans for 4–6 minutes or until just tender.
2 Heat the oil in a pan and gently fry the onion for 4–6 minutes or until just soft.
3 Mix the spices with a little water to make a paste. Add to the onions and cook for 2 minutes. Stir in the tomatoes.
4 Mix the yogurt with the cornflour and stir into the sauce. If it curdles, beat the sauce over a high heat.
5 Add the beans and season to taste.
6 For the pancakes, blend the milk, egg and oil together for 30 seconds in a blender or food processor. Add the flour and salt and blend again to make a smooth batter.
7 Heat a little oil in a small frying pan and fry 2–3 tbsp (30–45ml) of batter for 2–3 minutes on each side to make 8–10 pancakes.
8 Fill each pancake with bean sauce, fold up and serve immediately with natural yogurt.

Wholemeal pancakes with a spicy bean filling

Split pea and potato pancakes

SPLIT PEA AND POTATO PANCAKES

INGREDIENTS

- 4 tsp (20ml) sunflower oil
- 2 onions, finely chopped
- 1 clove garlic, crushed
- 1 tsp (5ml) ground cumin
- 1 tsp (5ml) mustard powder
- 4oz (125g) green split peas
- 1oz (25g) sunflower seeds
- ½ pint (300ml) water
- 6oz (175g) potatoes, diced
- 2 tbsp (30ml) chopped fresh parsley
- 1 bay leaf
- 1 quantity of wholemeal batter (see p.80)
- 7oz can (200g) chopped tomatoes
- salt and pepper

GARNISH
- chopped fresh parsley

Illustrated left

Split peas and sunflower seeds make a nutritious pancake filling.

PREPARATION TIME: 40 mins (plus 40 mins for the peas)

COOKING TIME: 15 mins (plus 30 mins for the pancakes)

MAKES: 8–10 pancakes

METHOD

1 For the filling, fry one onion and the garlic for 5 minutes. Add the cumin, mustard, split peas and sunflower seeds. Cook for a further 5 minutes. Add the water, potato, parsley and a bay leaf. Boil, cover and simmer for 40 minutes. Meanwhile, make the pancakes (see p.80).

2 Remove the bay leaf and season. Put 2 tbsp (30ml) of filling on each pancake and roll up. Arrange on an ovenproof dish. Cover with foil. Heat in a preheated oven at Gas Mark 4, 350°F, 180°C for 15 minutes.

3 Meanwhile for the sauce, fry the other onion for 5 minutes. Add the tomatoes, boil, then simmer for 10 minutes. Season and purée. Pour over the pancakes and serve garnished with parsley.

SALAD LEAVES

*A*ll salad leaves are low in calories and high in vitamins and minerals, especially Vitamins A and C and folic acid. Always buy firm, fresh-looking lettuces and wash thoroughly before eating.

CHICORY

Obtainable through the winter, chicory is crisp and slightly bitter. Choose the whitest available.

RED CABBAGE

A winter vegetable, red cabbage adds vivid colour, a crunchy texture and Vitamin C to a green salad.

WATERCRESS

More than just a garnish, watercress lends a peppery flavour to summer salads and boosts the calcium and folic acid content.

CHINESE LEAVES

This lightly crunchy salad of Chinese origin is found all year round. It should be handled gently.

FRISÉ
(curly endive)

Known as chicory in America and chicoré in France, the slightly sharp-tasting, spiky leaves make an attractive salad base and add vitamins and minerals.

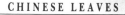

SPINACH

Rich in iron and folic acid, spinach makes a sharp, nutritious salad leaf.

OAKLEAF LETTUCE

Feuille de chêne is an appealing, jagged-leaved, heartless lettuce from France.

ICEBERG LETTUCE

The crispest and sweetest of lettuces, iceberg is also densely packed, so that the quantity of salad compensates for the higher price.

RADICCHIO

This Italian red chicory is high in folic acid and adds colour and a slightly bitter flavour to salads.

NASTURTIUM LEAVES

The leaves of this common garden plant make an unusual, delicately-flavoured addition to salads.

GARDEN CRESS

Often sown with mustard, cress is a fast-sprouting, fresh-tasting ingredient, easily grown at home.

COS LETTUCE

Cos or romaine lettuce, which is slightly sharper and coarser than other varieties, is available year-round.

ROUND LETTUCE

The standard, round lettuce is always available, but with more plentiful supplies in the summer. It should have a large, firm heart and unblemished leaves.

DAIRY PRODUCE

The availability of low-fat cheeses and milks means that "dairy products" can contribute protein, calcium and Vitamins A and D to a healthy diet without adding extra saturated fat. Keep cheeses and milk in the fridge, sealed from the air, and eat soft and curd cheeses and yogurt soon after purchase.

MOZZARELLA CHEESE

A famous, mild, Italian cheese; the traditional pizza topping.

CHÈVRE
(goat's cheese)

The name "chèvre" means goat and there are many varieties. Generally mild but tangy, these cheeses have an excellent mineral balance.

SKIMMED MILK

With the cream skimmed off, this milk contains only 0.1 per cent fat, while it retains all the water-soluble vitamins and minerals of whole milk.

SMETANA

An excellent, low-fat substitute for cream, smetana is a soured mixture of single cream and skimmed milk and contains 5–10 per cent fat.

PARMESAN CHEESE

A hard, grainy-textured cheese, made from scalded salted curd pressed for 2–5 years. It is used grated.

NATURAL YOGURT

A very good source of high quality protein, Vitamin B_2 and calcium. Easily digestible and ideal as a cream substitute.

SKIMMED MILK SOFT CHEESE/ QUARK

Made from semi-skimmed or skimmed milk, quark is a smooth, salt-free cheese with a slightly sharp taste.

RICOTTA

This low-fat, unripened Italian soft cheese is made from the whey, not the curds of cow's or goat's milk.

COTTAGE CHEESE

This low-fat, granular cheese is made from the separated curds of skimmed milk and is excellent with salads and fruit. A half-fat variety is also available.

CHEDDAR CHEESE

Cheddar is also available in reduced-fat and rennet-free forms. It is rich in protein, vitamins and minerals.

FROMAGE FRAIS

This non-fermented, non-cured, unsalted cheese is made from cooked goat's or cow's milk and cream. Varieties with a very low fat content are available.

BUTTERMILK

The residue from butter-making, this is similar to milk but with less fat and Vitamin A.

CURD CHEESE

Made from the separated curds of whole cow's milk and set without rennet, curd cheese contains 11 per cent fat and has a slightly acid flavour.

LIGHT
MAIN COURSES

ONION PIZZA TART   90
RICOTTA ROULADE   90
STUFFED MUSHROOMS   91
EGGS FLORENTINE   91
CHICORY WITH YOGURT HOLLANDAISE SAUCE   92
HERB GNOCCHI   92
AUBERGINE CHARLOTTE   93
PEASE PUDDING   93
TRADITIONAL BAKED BEANS   95
RED BEANS WITH SOURED CREAM   95
TOMATOES AND BASIL WITH A CRISP POTATO TOPPING   95
MAKING POTATO TOPPINGS   96
MUSHROOMS BAKED WITH OREGANO   96
RED CABBAGE WITH BEETROOT   96
CHEESE AND HERB BALLS   97

FROM TOP: Ricotta roulade (see p.90); Stuffed mushrooms (see p.91); Onion pizza tart (see p.90)

ONION PIZZA TART

INGREDIENTS

DOUGH
- 1 tsp (5ml) fresh yeast
- 3 tbsp (45ml) warm water
- 1 egg, beaten
- 4oz (125g) wholemeal flour
- ½ tsp salt

TOPPING
- 1 tbsp (15ml) olive oil
- 2 large onions, peeled and finely chopped
- 2 tsp (10ml) chopped fresh basil
- salt and black pepper
- 4 tomatoes, sliced
- 16 black olives, stoned
- 12 fresh basil leaves

Illustrated on page 89

Sometimes known as pissaladière, this French dish is a cross between onion tart and pizza. This low-fat version is light enough to be served as a starter before a salad or vegetable main course. If you do not have basil, try using oregano or marjoram instead.

PREPARATION TIME: 30 mins (plus 35 mins rising time for the dough)
COOKING TIME: 40–55 mins
SERVES 4

METHOD

1 Mix the yeast with warm water. Leave to stand for 5 minutes in a warm place.
2 Add the beaten egg to the yeast mixture. Put the flour and salt in a bowl and make a well in the centre. Add the yeast mixture and mix together to a soft dough (add extra water if necessary).
3 Turn the dough on to a floured board and knead for 5 minutes until smooth and elastic.
4 Transfer the dough to a clean bowl. Cover with clingfilm and leave to rise for 35 minutes in a warm place.
5 For the topping, heat the oil in a saucepan and fry the onions on a low heat for 20–25 minutes until soft and almost puréed. Add the chopped basil and seasoning.
6 When the dough has risen, knock it back and knead lightly. Roll out the dough to fit a greased 8-inch (20cm) flan ring. Push the dough well into the sides.
7 Spread over the onion mixture. Arrange the tomatoes on top and add the olives in a decorative pattern. Season with pepper.
8 Leave to prove for a further 10–15 minutes. Bake in a preheated oven at Gas Mark 5, 375°F, 190°C for 20–30 minutes.
9 When cooked, cool slightly and arrange the basil leaves on top. Serve hot or warm.

RICOTTA ROULADE

INGREDIENTS
- 6oz (175g) spinach
- 1 tsp (5ml) made mustard
- 3 eggs, separated
- salt and black pepper

FILLING
- 6oz (175g) fresh ricotta cheese, mashed

GARNISH
- sprig of coriander

Illustrated on page 89

Spinach is rich in iron and has a strong flavour that balances well with ricotta cheese.

PREPARATION TIME: 35 mins
COOKING TIME: 15–20 mins
SERVES 4

METHOD

1 Wash the spinach thoroughly. Put it in a saucepan with only the water on its leaves and cook for about 10 minutes.
2 When cooked, cool slightly and drain thoroughly. Chop the leaves as finely as possible. Transfer the chopped leaves to a mixing bowl, add the mustard and egg yolks and then season. Carefully fold the stiffly whisked egg whites into the mixture.
3 Pour into a lined Swiss roll tin, and bake in a preheated oven at Gas Mark 6, 400°F, 200°C for 15–20 minutes or until golden brown and starting to shrink from the sides of the tin.
4 Leave to cool for 2–3 minutes, then turn it out on to a sheet of greaseproof paper and carefully peel off the lining paper. Cover with the mashed ricotta and roll up.
5 Reduce the oven to Gas Mark 5, 375°F, 190°C and reheat the roulade quickly for 5 minutes.
6 Trim off the ends and serve in slices.

STUFFED MUSHROOMS

INGREDIENTS

- 4 large flat mushrooms, wiped
- 1 tbsp (15ml) olive oil
- 3–4 shallots or 1 small onion, peeled and finely chopped
- 1 clove garlic, crushed
- 8oz (250g) large flat mushrooms, chopped
- 5 tbsp (75ml) red wine
- ½ tsp dried thyme
- 1 tbsp (15ml) tomato purée

GARNISH
- sprig of parsley

Illustrated on page 89

These stuffed mushrooms, filled with a classic 'Duxelles' sauce of mushrooms, wine and shallots or onions, make a light main course.

PREPARATION TIME: 25 mins
COOKING TIME: 20–25 mins
SERVES 4

METHOD

1 Remove the stalks from the 4 large flat mushrooms and chop the stalks finely. Put the caps on one side. Heat 2 tsp (10ml) of the oil in a medium-sized frying pan and fry the stalks, onion, garlic and chopped mushrooms for 5–10 minutes or until very soft.
2 Mix in the red wine and thyme and continue cooking until the wine has almost evaporated. Stir in the tomato purée and seasoning and cook for 2–3 minutes.
3 Place the flat mushroom caps in a greased dish. Brush the rest of the oil on to the caps, and pile on the filling. Bake in a preheated oven at Gas Mark 5, 375°F, 190°C for 20–25 minutes.

EGGS FLORENTINE

INGREDIENTS

- 1 tsp (5ml) butter or margarine
- 8 spinach leaves, chopped in strips
- 4 fl oz (125 ml) soured cream or smetana
- 4 eggs
- salt and black pepper

GARNISH
- chopped fresh parsley

Illustrated right

Served in ramekin dishes surrounded by small wholemeal toasts, this makes an attractive, nutritious light lunch.

PREPARATION TIME: 10 mins
COOKING TIME: 25 MINS
SERVES 4

METHOD

1 Grease 4 ramekin dishes with the butter. Divide half the spinach and put into the base of each ramekin dish. Add 1 tsp (5ml) soured cream or smetana and break an egg into each.
2 Arrange the rest of the spinach over the egg whites and cover with the rest of the soured cream or smetana, leaving the yolks bare. Season.
3 Bake in a preheated oven at Gas Mark 4, 350°F, 180°C for 25 minutes or until the egg is just about to set. Serve immediately.

CLOCKWISE FROM TOP LEFT: Eggs florentine; Chicory with yogurt hollandaise sauce (see p.92); Herb gnocchi (see p.92)

CHICORY WITH YOGURT HOLLANDAISE SAUCE

INGREDIENTS

■ 4 heads of chicory (about 1lb/500g in weight)
■ 1 tsp (5ml) butter or margarine
■ salt and black pepper
■ 4 spinach leaves

SAUCE
■ 2 tbsp (30ml) wine vinegar
■ 4 black peppercorns
■ 1 bay leaf
■ 1 blade mace
■ 2 egg yolks
■ 4 fl oz (125ml) natural yogurt

Illustrated on page 91

This hollandaise sauce, which uses yogurt instead of butter, is a low-calorie version of the traditional recipe. Take care not to overheat the sauce or it will curdle. Serve warm.

PREPARATION TIME: 25 mins
COOKING TIME: 1 hour
SERVES 4

METHOD

1 Trim the stems of the chicory and discard any wilted outside leaves. Arrange in a lightly buttered ovenproof dish. Season.
2 Cover and bake in a preheated oven at Gas Mark 4, 350°F, 180°C for 50 minutes. Roll each chicory head in a spinach leaf, cover with foil and cook for a further 10 minutes.
3 For the hollandaise sauce, mix the wine vinegar, peppercorns, bay leaf and mace in a saucepan and bring to the boil. Continue boiling until the liquid has reduced to 2 tsp (10ml).
4 Beat the egg yolks in a small bowl. Strain the reduced vinegar into them. Put the bowl over a pan of hot water and heat gently, stirring constantly, until thickened. Add the yogurt, season and continue stirring until the sauce coats the back of the spoon.
5 Drain the chicory and serve with the sauce poured over.

HERB GNOCCHI

INGREDIENTS

■ 2oz (50g) fresh watercress leaves
■ 6oz (175g) spinach leaves
■ ½oz (15g) fresh parsley
■ 2 tsp (10ml) fresh tarragon, finely chopped
■ 2 tsp (10ml) fresh marjoram, finely chopped
■ 2oz ricotta cheese
■ 2oz (50g) curd cheese
■ 1 size 6 egg, beaten
■ 1½oz (40g) semolina

GARNISH
■ Parmesan cheese, grated

Illustrated on page 91

This is a low-fat version of Italian gnocchi. Here the semolina dumplings are flavoured with spinach, watercress and fresh herbs.

PREPARATION TIME: 25 mins
COOKING TIME: 25 mins
SERVES 4—5

METHOD

1 Wash and steam the watercress leaves, spinach and parsley together for 6–10 minutes. Drain and dry well, chop finely, then place in a bowl and stir in the herbs.
2 Mix together the ricotta cheese, curd cheese and egg in a separate bowl. Mix well and add to the chopped herbs and vegetables. Stir in the semolina and leave to cool thoroughly.
3 Bring a saucepan of water to the boil. Gently drop 4–6 dessertspoonsful of the mixture at a time into the the simmering water and cook until the gnocchi rise to the surface.
4 Remove from the pan using a slotted spoon and place on a serving dish. Sprinkle on some Parmesan cheese and serve hot.

Aubergine charlotte

AUBERGINE CHARLOTTE

INGREDIENTS

- 3 small aubergines (about 1–1¼lb/ 500–625g in weight)
- 1 tsp (5ml) salt
- 2 tbsp (30ml) olive oil
- 1 medium onion, peeled and finely chopped
- 1 clove garlic, crushed
- 2 tsp (10ml) fresh basil
- 8 tomatoes, skinned and chopped
- salt and black pepper
- ½ pint (300ml) natural set yogurt
- 1 tsp (5ml) ground cumin
- 2oz (50g) walnuts

GARNISH

- 1oz (25g) shelled walnuts, finely chopped

Illustrated left

This recipe makes an impressive layered galette, which can taste even better cold than hot.

PREPARATION TIME: 50 mins
COOKING TIME: 50 mins
SERVES 4

METHOD

1 Trim the aubergines and cut the flesh into ½-inch (1cm) slices. Sprinkle them with salt and leave for 30 minutes to get rid of the excess bitter juices. Rinse with cold water and dry thoroughly.
2 Heat 2 tsp (10ml) olive oil in a saucepan and fry the onion until soft. Add the garlic and basil and cook for a further 2–3 minutes.
3 Stir in the tomatoes. Cook for 20–25 minutes until the mixture resembles a thick pulp. Season to taste.
4 Brush one side of the aubergine slices with oil and cook under a preheated grill until golden brown. Turn them over and cook on the other side. Leave to cool.
5 Mix the yogurt and cumin together until smooth.
6 Grease a 2-pint (1.2-litre) capacity charlotte mould or a 7-inch (18cm) round cake tin, and arrange a layer of overlapping aubergine slices at the bottom of the dish.
7 Reserve a third of the tomato mixture. Spread some of the remaining tomato mixture over the aubergines, sprinkle with some walnuts, then add some of the yogurt mixture. Repeat the layers, finishing with a layer of aubergine slices.
8 Cover the mould with foil and bake in a preheated oven at Gas Mark 4, 350°F, 180°C for 40–50 minutes or until the aubergines are tender.
9 Cool in the dish and turn out when required. Serve with the remaining tomato sauce spooned over and garnished with chopped nuts.

PEASE PUDDING

INGREDIENTS

- 8oz (250g) yellow or green split peas
- 1 onion, peeled and cut into quarters
- 1 parsnip, scrubbed and roughly chopped
- 4oz (125g) celeriac, peeled and roughly chopped
- sprigs of parsley and thyme
- 1½–2 pints (900ml–1.2 litres) water
- 1oz (25g) margarine
- 2 tbsp (30ml) finely chopped fresh parsley
- 1 tsp (5ml) dried thyme
- salt and black pepper

Illustrated on page 94

Pease pudding is a delicious, warming winter dish. The peas are cooked in a stock full of vegetables so that they become well flavoured. Once cooked, the purée is enriched with margarine, which prevents the end result from being too dry, and either served immediately or baked to become slightly firm. If you prefer a firmer texture, you could beat in an egg and then steam the pudding for 30 minutes. Serve pease pudding with baked jacket potatoes or rice for a simple supper, or serve small portions with a grain or nut roast.

PREPARATION TIME: 10 mins
COOKING TIME: 20-25 mins (plus 40–50 mins for the peas)
SERVES 4

METHOD

1 Place the peas in a large pan with the onion, parsnip, celeriac, sprigs of parsley and thyme, and water. Bring to the boil, cover and simmer for 40–45 minutes. Drain and remove the vegetables and herbs.
2 Put the peas back into the pan and beat well to form into a purée. Add the margarine and herbs. Season well.
3 For a soft pudding, serve immediately. Alternatively, spoon into a lightly greased 9-inch (23cm) square ovenproof dish. Bake in a preheated oven at Gas Mark 4, 350°F, 180°C for 20–25 minutes.

TRADITIONAL BAKED BEANS

INGREDIENTS

- 4oz (125g) haricot beans, soaked
- 1 tbsp (15ml) sunflower oil
- 1 onion, peeled and finely chopped
- 2 cloves garlic, crushed
- 2 tbsp (30ml) apple juice
- 4 slices lemon
- 14oz (400g) can tomatoes, puréed.
- 1 tbsp (15ml) wholegrain mustard
- 1 tbsp (15ml) black treacle or molasses
- ½ tsp ground cumin
- pinch chilli powder
- salt and pepper

Illustrated left

Traditionally the beans were cooked for several hours in a slow oven, but it is easier and quicker to cook them first and then stew them in the sauce for a short time.

PREPARATION TIME : 10 mins (plus 10–12 hours soaking time)

COOKING TIME: 30–40 mins (plus 40–45 mins for the beans)

SERVES 2–4

METHOD

1 Drain the beans. Bring to the boil in plenty of fresh water. Boil fast for 10 minutes, then cover and simmer for 30-35 minutes or until cooked. Drain well.
2 Heat the oil and gently cook the onion and garlic until soft. Add the remaining ingredients including the cooked beans. Simmer uncovered for 30-40 minutes, stirring occasionally. Season to taste and serve hot or cold.

Tomatoes and basil with a crisp potato topping

RED BEANS WITH SOURED CREAM

INGREDIENTS

- 4oz (125g) red kidney beans, soaked
- 2 tsp (10ml) olive oil
- 4oz (125g) small pickling onions
- 3 cloves garlic, crushed
- 2 large red peppers, deseeded and diced
- 2 tsp (10ml) cumin seeds
- 2 tsp (10ml) dried oregano
- juice of 1 orange
- salt and pepper
- ¼ pint (150ml) soured cream or smetana

Illustrated left

A simple bean recipe that goes well with rice dishes, vegetable bakes or nut roasts.

PREPARATION TIME: 20 mins (plus 10–12 hours soaking time)

COOKING TIME: 20 mins (plus 50 mins for the beans)

SERVES 4

METHOD

1 Drain the beans. Place in a pan with plenty of fresh water. Bring to the boil and boil fast for 10 minutes, then cover and simmer for 30–40 minutes. Drain well.
2 Heat the oil in a pan and gently fry the onions until soft. Add the garlic, red peppers, cooked beans and cumin seeds. Cover and cook for 10–12 minutes, stirring occasionally.
3 Stir in the oregano and orange juice and cook for 5 minutes. Season well. Transfer to a warmed serving dish and cover with soured cream or smetana before serving.

TOMATOES AND BASIL WITH A CRISP POTATO TOPPING

INGREDIENTS

- 1lb (500g) potatoes, sliced
- ½oz (15g) margarine
- 2–3 tbsp (30–45ml) skimmed milk
- ¼ tsp black pepper
- 14oz (400g) can of tomatoes, drained
- 2 tsp (10ml) chopped fresh basil
- 2oz (50g) Cheddar cheese, grated

Illustrated above

Serve these creamy potatoes with a root-, shoot- or fruit-based salad. If you like a decorative finish, try piping the potato on the top.

PREPARATION TIME: 30 mins

COOKING TIME: 25 mins

SERVES 4

METHOD

1 Cover the potatoes with plenty of cold water. Bring to the boil, cover and simmer for 15–20 minutes or until soft. Drain, add the margarine, milk and black pepper and mash.
2 Place the tomatoes in an ovenproof dish. Sprinkle with basil, top with mashed potato, then sprinkle with the grated cheese.
3 Bake in a preheated oven at Gas Mark 5, 375°F, 190°C for 25 minutes until golden brown.

FROM TOP: Traditional baked beans; Pease pudding (see p.93); Red beans with soured cream

MAKING POTATO TOPPINGS

*P*otatoes are one of the most versatile vegetables. Certain cooking methods like baking in jackets or boiling in skins are the most nutritious ways of preparing them. Mashed potato makes an attractive and tasty topping. The mixture should be smooth and moist, but peel the potatoes only if you want to pipe them.

1 Use 2 dessertspoons of mashed potato to make oval potato cakes. Place on top of the dish.

2 Use a star-shaped nozzle and piping bag to pipe small spirals of potato in rows across the dish.

3 Place a layer of potato over the vegetables and decorate with the back of a fork.

MUSHROOMS BAKED WITH OREGANO

INGREDIENTS

- 8oz (250g) flat mushrooms
- 2 tbsp (30ml) lemon juice
- 1 tbsp (15ml) soya sauce
- 1 tbsp (15ml) tomato purée
- 1 clove garlic, crushed
- 2 tsp (10ml) chopped fresh oregano
- ½ tsp black pepper
- 3 fl oz (75ml) water
- 1 tsp (5ml) olive oil

Illustrated right

Flat mushrooms are button mushrooms that have been allowed to develop and open their caps. Baked slowly in a well-flavoured stock, they make a delicious accompaniment to a vegetable risotto.

PREPARATION TIME: 10 mins
COOKING TIME: 30 mins
SERVES 4

METHOD

1 Arrange the mushrooms in the base of a large casserole.
2 Mix together the lemon juice, soya sauce, tomato purée, garlic, oregano, black pepper and water. Pour on to the mushrooms and brush lightly with the olive oil.
3 Cover the casserole and bake in a preheated oven at Gas Mark 4, 350°F, 180°C for 30 minutes. Serve hot or cold.

RED CABBAGE WITH BEETROOT

INGREDIENTS

- 2 tsp (10ml) olive oil
- 12oz (375g) red cabbage, shredded
- 6oz (175g) raw beetroot, coarsely grated
- 1 large onion, finely chopped
- 1 clove garlic, crushed
- 2 tbsp (30ml) soya sauce
- 2 tbsp (30ml) apple juice
- 3 tbsp (45ml) cider vinegar

Illustrated right

With their complementary flavours and colour, beetroot and red cabbage make an attractive combination, especially when topped with a little natural yogurt. Try serving this as an accompaniment to egg dishes, such as a soufflé or an omelette.

PREPARATION TIME: 25 mins
COOKING TIME: 10 mins
SERVES 4

METHOD

1 Heat the oil in a large frying pan. Cover and gently fry the cabbage, beetroot, onion and garlic for 10–15 minutes stirring frequently.
2 Mix the soya sauce, apple juice and cider vinegar together. Pour over the vegetables. Continue cooking gently for a further 10 minutes. Serve hot or cold.

FROM TOP: Mushrooms baked with oregano; Red cabbage with beetroot

Cheese and herb balls

CHEESE AND HERB BALLS

INGREDIENTS

■ 8oz (250g) curd cheese
■ 2 tbsp (30ml) peanuts, finely chopped
■ 1 clove garlic, crushed
■ 4 spring onions, trimmed and finely chopped
■ 1 tbsp (15ml) chopped fresh parsley
■ 1 tbsp (15ml) chopped fresh chives
■ 1 tbsp (15ml) chopped fresh tarragon
■ salt and pepper

COATING

■ 1oz (25g) unsalted peanuts, ground

Illustrated above

The firm texture of curd cheese is ideal as a base for savoury or sweet balls. Fresh herbs and nuts add extra nutrients as well as flavour. Alternatively, you could create your own variations by adding spices, seeds or dried fruits. This dish looks attractive served on a bed of frisé and garnished with sliced cherry tomatoes.

PREPARATION TIME: 15 mins
SERVES 4

METHOD

1 In a food processor or blender, mix the curd cheese with the chopped peanuts and garlic.
2 Add the finely chopped spring onions and herbs, mix well. Season to taste.
3 Shape into small balls and coat in the ground peanuts.

SALADS

CRUNCHY NUT SALAD WITH CHICORY	100
NUT SALAD CREOLE	100
ALMOND AND FENNEL SALAD	100
HAZELNUT WALDORF	100
BUTTER BEAN SALAD WITH CREAMY DRESSING	101
FIVE BEAN SALAD	101
WALDORF SALAD	101
FRUIT SALAD COCKTAIL WITH CURRIED MAYONNAISE	102
SPIKY BEETROOT SALAD WITH AVOCADO DRESSING	102
SPANISH SALAD WITH TOMATO DRESSING	103
GREEK SALAD	103
AUTUMN MEDLEY	103
MUSHROOM SALAD WITH MINTY HORSERADISH SAUCE	104
TRADITIONAL COLESLAW WITH YOGURT AND MUSTARD DRESSING	104
BEETROOT SLAW WITH ORANGE DRESSING	105
CREAMED CELERIAC SALAD	105
RED CABBAGE SLAW WITH A SWEET AND SOUR DRESSING	105
CLASSIC GREEN SALAD	106
CHICORY AND GRAPEFRUIT SALAD	106
TOMATO AND ORANGE SALAD WITH NUTMEG DRESSING	106
CALIFORNIAN SALAD WITH TARRAGON DRESSING	107
FRUIT AND FENNEL SALAD	107
LOW-CALORIE MAYONNAISE	108
AIOLI	108
LIGHT MAYONNAISE	109
HERB MAYONNAISE	109
CLASSIC MAYONNAISE	109
CURRIED MAYONNAISE	109

FROM TOP: Crunchy nut salad with chicory (see p.100); Hazelnut waldorf (see p.100); Nut salad creole (see p.100); Almond and fennel salad (see p.100)

CRUNCHY NUT SALAD WITH CHICORY

INGREDIENTS

- 1oz (25g) cashew nuts
- 1oz (25g) Brazil nuts
- 4oz (125g) chicory, sliced
- 1 yellow pepper, deseeded and diced
- 1 punnet salad cress
- 4oz (125g) green seedless grapes
- juice of ½ an orange
- 1 tbsp (15ml) olive oil
- 2 tsp (10ml) fresh tarragon

Illustrated on page 99

An exotic salad of mixed, creamy nuts contrasted with crisp, salad vegetables and juicy grapes. Served with a whole grain such as rice or buckwheat, this recipe is a good source of protein.

PREPARATION TIME: 20 mins

SERVES 4

METHOD

1 Lightly toast the nuts under the grill for 2–3 minutes.
2 Mix the chicory, pepper, cress and grapes together in a bowl. Stir in the nuts.
3 For the dressing, mix together the orange juice, oil and tarragon and season to taste. Pour over the salad.

NUT SALAD CREOLE

INGREDIENTS

- 2 oranges
- 2 large bananas, sliced
- 1oz (25g) fresh coconut, grated
- 2oz (50g) unsalted peanuts

DRESSING

- 1 tbsp (15ml) sunflower oil
- 3 tbsp (45ml) lemon juice
- 1 tsp (5ml) clear honey

Illustrated on page 99

This salad is good as an accompaniment for savoury dishes, or as a sweet starter or dessert. It tastes best made with fresh coconut; shake it to check that there is milk inside — the more liquid, the fresher the coconut. Pineapple could be used instead.

PREPARATION TIME: 25 mins

SERVES 4

METHOD

1 Peel and segment the oranges, reserving the juice.
2 Mix the banana slices and grated coconut with the orange slices and juice.
3 Lightly toast the peanuts for 3–4 minutes under the grill, then rub off the skins and roughly chop. Mix into the salad.
4 For the dressing, mix the ingredients together and pour over the salad.

ALMOND AND FENNEL SALAD

INGREDIENTS

DRESSING

- ¾oz (20g) ground almonds
- 2 small cloves garlic
- pinch chilli powder
- pinch salt
- 2 tsp (10ml) tomato purée
- 1 tbsp (15ml) red wine vinegar
- 2–4 fl oz (50–125ml) olive oil

SALAD

- 8oz (250g) fennel, diced
- 1 large red pepper, deseeded and diced
- 8oz (250g) young courgettes, diced
- 2oz (50g) blanched almonds

Illustrated on page 99

Nut creams make good alternatives to mayonnaise and also provide a high-protein dressing for salads. Fennel, red pepper and courgettes all have a crisp texture and excellent flavour.

PREPARATION TIME: 30 mins

SERVES 4

METHOD

1 For the dressing, mix the almonds with the garlic, chilli powder, salt, tomato purée and vinegar in a blender or food processor.
2 Gradually add the oil, 1 tsp (5ml) at a time, blending very well to prevent the mixture from curdling.
3 When half the oil has been added pour in the rest in a slow stream until the dressing is thick and creamy.
4 For the salad, prepare the vegetables and toss together in a large bowl.
5 Lightly toast the almonds under a preheated grill for 2–3 minutes, then chop roughly and mix in with the vegetables.
6 Pour the dressing over the salad and toss.

HAZELNUT WALDORF

INGREDIENTS

- 4–6oz (125–175g) hazelnuts
- 2 large sticks celery, sliced diagonally
- 2 red-skinned apples, cored and chopped
- 4oz (125g) fennel, diced

DRESSING

- 4oz (125g) skimmed milk soft cheese (quark)
- juice of ½ a lemon
- 3 tsp (15ml) sunflower oil
- 2 tsp (10ml) chopped fresh mint

Illustrated on page 99

This high-protein salad makes a good, light meal when served with wholemeal bread. The crunchy texture of nuts, celery, apples and fennel is well complemented by the creamy dressing.

PREPARATION TIME: 25 mins

SERVES 4

METHOD

1 Lightly toast the hazelnuts under the grill, or in a moderate oven, for several minutes. Rub off the skins, using a cloth.
2 Prepare the celery, apples and fennel. Mix together with the hazelnuts.
3 For the dressing, blend all the ingredients together until smooth. Mix into the salad. Serve on crisp red radicchio or green lettuce.

FROM TOP: Butter bean salad with creamy dressing; Five bean salad

BUTTER BEAN SALAD WITH CREAMY DRESSING

INGREDIENTS

- 4oz (125g) butter beans, soaked
- 2 cloves garlic
- 1 bay leaf
- 8 tomatoes, sliced
- 1 punnet salad cress

DRESSING

- 4 tbsp (60ml) natural yogurt
- 2 tbsp (30ml) soured cream or smetana
- 1 tbsp (15ml) olive oil
- 1 tbsp (15ml) white wine vinegar
- 1 tbsp (15ml) chopped fresh basil
- 1 tsp (5ml) grated (or 2 tsp/10ml creamed) horseradish
- salt and pepper

Illustrated above

Butter beans have a mild flavour, which becomes stronger when garlic, herbs or vegetables are added to the cooking water. They make a delicious salad with juicy tomatoes and a strongly-flavoured creamy dressing. For a slightly nuttier flavour, try using lima beans which are very similar in appearance to butter beans, but smaller.

PREPARATION TIME: 10 mins (plus 10–12 hours soaking time)

COOKING TIME: 40–50 mins for the beans

SERVES 4

METHOD

1 Drain the beans. Bring to the boil in plenty of fresh water with the crushed garlic and a bay leaf. Boil fast for 10 minutes, then cover and simmer for 30–40 minutes or until tender. Drain and cool.
2 Remove the bay leaf. Mix the beans with the tomatoes and cress.
3 For the dressing, mix all the ingredients together and toss into the salad. Season.

FIVE BEAN SALAD

INGREDIENTS

- 1lb (500g) broad beans
- 1lb (500g) French beans
- 1lb (500g) cooked haricot beans
- 1lb (500g) cooked chick peas
- 1lb (500g) cooked red kidney beans
- 12 large spring onions, diced
- 10oz (300g) radishes, sliced
- 4 avocados, peeled and diced
- 8 tbsp (120ml) chopped parsley

DRESSING

- 8 tbsp (120ml) sunflower oil
- 8 tbsp (120ml) cider vinegar
- 4 tsp (20ml) wholegrain mustard
- 2 green chillies, deseeded and diced

Illustrated left

This is an excellent party dish as you can cook large quantities of the pulses at a time, marinate them in the dressing while they are still freshly cooked, then refrigerate until required. However, if you only want to make enough for 4 servings, 2oz (50g) dry weight of each pulse will give about 4oz (125g) when cooked. To cook chick peas, see page 9. Cook the other pulses in the same way, but simmer for 30 minutes only.

PREPARATION TIME: 25 mins

SERVES 16

METHOD

1 Steam the broad beans and French beans for 4–5 minutes
2 Mix the fresh beans with the cooked haricot beans, chick peas and red kidney beans.
3 Stir in the spring onions, radishes, avocados and parsley.
4 For the dressing, combine the ingredients and season well.
5 Pour the dressing over the salad and toss well.

WALDORF SALAD

INGREDIENTS

- 4 sticks of celery, trimmed
- 4oz (125g) fresh dates, stoned
- 2 red apples
- 2oz (50g) Cheddar cheese
- 6 tbsp (90ml) mayonnaise
- 6 tbsp (90ml) natural yogurt
- 1 tsp (5ml) caraway seeds
- 12 walnut halves
- salt and pepper

GARNISH

- celery leaf

Illustrated on page 102

The caraway not only lifts the flavour, but helps the digestion of the rich dressing. If you use Cheddar, slice it thinly so that it goes a long way. If you want to reduce the fat and calorie content, use a low-calorie mayonnaise and low-fat cheese.

PREPARATION TIME: 20 mins

SERVES 4

METHOD

1 Cut the celery on the diagonal into coarse pieces.
2 Roughly chop the dates and apples.
3 Cut the cheese into very thin slices.
4 Mix together the mayonnaise, yogurt, caraway seeds and walnut halves. Combine all the ingredients. Season to taste and garnish with the celery leaf.

FRUIT SALAD COCKTAIL WITH CURRIED MAYONNAISE

INGREDIENTS

- ½ pineapple
- 1lb (500g) watermelon, peeled
- 2oz (50g) bean sprouts
- ¼ cucumber

DRESSING

- 4 tbsp (60ml) curried mayonnaise (see page 109)

Illustrated left

Clean but spicy, a savoury fruit salad makes a refreshing low-calorie accompaniment to a bean or nut dip.
PREPARATION TIME: 20 mins
SERVES 4

METHOD

1 Peel the fruit and cut into coarse chunks.
2 Rinse the bean sprouts.
3 Cut the cucumber into chunks.
4 Mix all the ingredients together in a large bowl and stir in the dressing.

SPIKY BEETROOT SALAD WITH AVOCADO DRESSING

INGREDIENTS

- 4 large sticks celery, trimmed
- 8oz (250g) raw beetroot, peeled
- 8oz (250g) carrots, peeled
- juice of ½ lemon
- 1 tsp (5ml) honey

DRESSING

- 1 avocado, peeled and stoned
- juice of 1 large lemon
- 2 tbsp (30ml) natural yogurt
- 2 cloves garlic, crushed
- 1 tsp (5ml) honey
- salt and pepper

GARNISH

- coriander leaf
- lamb's lettuce
- oakleaf lettuce

Illustrated left

It is worth trying raw beetroot — it has a distinctive flavour and is more nutritious than cooked. The sharp yet creamy avocado dressing balances and complements the crunchy texture of the three vegetables.
PREPARATION TIME: 25 mins
SERVES 4

METHOD

1 Cut the celery, beetroot and carrot into julienne strips.
2 Combine the lemon juice and honey.
3 Toss the beetroot and carrots separately in the mixture to keep them fresh.
4 For the dressing, blend the avocado with the remaining ingredients and garnish with a coriander leaf.
5 Arrange clusters of celery, beetroot and carrot strips clockwise around a large circular plate. Then garnish the centre of the plate with lamb's and oakleaf lettuce.

FROM TOP: Waldorf salad (see p.101); Fruit salad cocktail with curried mayonnaise; Spiky beetroot salad with (RIGHT) avocado dressing

SPANISH SALAD WITH TOMATO DRESSING

INGREDIENTS

- 1 small onion, peeled
- 1 green pepper, deseeded
- 4oz (125g) courgettes, wiped
- 1 small avocado, peeled
- 4 medium tomatoes

DRESSING

- 2 tomatoes, skinned and chopped
- 1 tbsp (15ml) tomato purée
- juice of ½ a lemon
- 1 tbsp (15ml) olive oil
- ½ tsp chopped fresh oregano
- ½ tsp chopped fresh thyme
- 2 cloves garlic, chopped

GARNISH

- sprig of oregano

Illustrated right

The light tomato dressing enhances the flavour of the vegetables and if you have any left over, try using it as a base for Gazpacho.

PREPARATION TIME: 25 mins
SERVES 4

METHOD

1 Slice the onion into very thin rings.
2 Cut the pepper into rings.
3 Cut the courgettes, avocado and tomatoes into fine slices.
4 For the dressing, blend the tomatoes, purée and lemon juice, then add the oil and herbs.
5 Mix in the garlic. Season to taste.
6 Toss all the salad ingredients together and pour the dressing over the top. Garnish with a sprig of oregano.

GREEK SALAD

INGREDIENTS

- 7oz (200g) feta cheese, cubed
- ½ cucumber, diced
- 20 fresh black olives, stoned and chopped
- 4 small tomatoes, halved
- 1 green pepper, deseeded and sliced into strips
- juice of 1 lemon

GARNISH

- sprig of mint

Illustrated right

The feta cheese makes this a substantial main course and its strong flavour is well complemented by the olives and the plain lemon juice dressing. Try serving with warm wholemeal pitta bread, for a balanced main course.

PREPARATION TIME: 15 mins
SERVES 4

METHOD

1 Prepare all the salad ingredients and mix together in a large bowl.
2 Toss in lemon juice and garnish with fresh mint.

AUTUMN MEDLEY

INGREDIENTS

- 6oz (175g) broccoli, trimmed
- 6oz (175g) fennel, trimmed
- 4oz (125g) turnip, scrubbed or peeled
- 6oz (175g) carrots, scrubbed or peeled
- 6oz (175g) Brussels sprouts, trimmed

DRESSING

- 4–5 tbsp (60–75ml) apple juice
- 2 tbsp (30ml) yogurt
- 1 tsp (5ml) lemon juice
- salt and pepper

Illustrated below

Winter vegetables, although not normally associated with salads, can be just as good raw as summer produce, and equally nutritious. Remember, however, to cut those with stronger flavours into small pieces as large chunks can be overpowering.

PREPARATION TIME: 25 mins
SERVES 4

METHOD

1 Cut the broccoli into small spears, the fennel into thin strips, the turnips and carrots into round slices and the sprouts into quarters and mix together in a large bowl.
2 For the dressing, mix the apple juice gradually into the yogurt, then add the remaining ingredients and season to taste.
3 Pour the dressing over the salad and mix thoroughly.

FROM TOP: Greek salad; Autumn medley; Spanish salad with tomato dressing

Mushroom salad with minty horseradish sauce

Traditional coleslaw with yogurt and mustard dressing

MUSHROOM SALAD WITH MINTY HORSERADISH SAUCE

INGREDIENTS

■ 12oz (375g) baby button mushrooms
■ 2 tbsp (30ml) creamed horseradish
■ 3–4 tbsp (45–60ml) natural yogurt
■ 1 tbsp (15ml) finely chopped fresh mint
■ salt and pepper

GARNISH
■ sprig of mint

Illustrated above

A simple, low calorie salad with a delicious subtle flavour and smooth texture. Wipe rather than wash the mushrooms, or you will lose valuable vitamins.

PREPARATION TIME: 15 mins
SERVES 4

METHOD

1 Carefully wipe the mushrooms with a damp cloth. Cut them into quarters, or if they are very small leave them whole.
2 Mix together the horseradish, yogurt and mint and season to taste. Mix into the mushrooms. Garnish with mint and serve.

TRADITIONAL COLESLAW WITH YOGURT AND MUSTARD DRESSING

INGREDIENTS

■ 8oz (250g) white cabbage, shredded
■ 4oz (125g) carrots, scrubbed and grated
■ 2oz (50g) unsalted peanuts
■ 3 spring onions, trimmed and coarsely chopped

DRESSING
■ 6 tbsp (90ml) mayonnaise
■ 6 tbsp (90ml) natural yogurt
■ 1 tsp (5ml) wholegrain mustard
■ salt and pepper

GARNISH
■ watercress

Illustrated above

The sweetness of carrots complements the crispness of cabbage and makes a good colour contrast. Peanuts add protein and texture and the onions and mustard sharpen the flavour. If you want to reduce the calorie content, use a low-calorie mayonnaise.

PREPARATION TIME: 25 mins
SERVES 4

METHOD

1 Prepare the cabbage and carrots. Mix well with the nuts and spring onions.
2 Mix the dressing ingredients together and toss into the salad.
3 Serve at room temperature on a bed of crisp lettuce, garnished with watercress.

BEETROOT SLAW WITH ORANGE DRESSING

INGREDIENTS

- 2oz (50g) raisins
- juice of ½ an orange
- 8–10oz (250–300g) raw baby beetroot, peeled
- 2 tbsp (30ml) finely chopped chives

DRESSING

- juice of 1½ oranges
- 1 tsp (5ml) orange rind
- 1 tbsp (15ml) sunflower oil
- 1 clove garlic, crushed
- salt and pepper

Illustrated right

Baby beetroots are sweet and delicious raw and have a flavour that blends well with the dried fruits. If you have time, soak the raisins in fruit juice for the best end results.

PREPARATION TIME: 20 mins (plus 1–2 hours soaking time)

SERVES 4

METHOD

1 Soak the raisins in orange juice for 1–2 hours.
2 Prepare the beetroot and grate finely.
3 Mix in the raisins and the chives.
4 For the dressing, mix the ingredients together and toss into the salad.

CREAMED CELERIAC SALAD

INGREDIENTS

- 8–10oz (250–300g) celeriac
- 1 red apple
- 2oz (50g) chopped mixed nuts
- 3–4 tbsp (45–60ml) soured cream or smetana
- juice of ½ a lemon
- pinch turmeric
- salt and pepper

Illustrated right

Celeriac may look ugly on the outside, but its skin masks a deliciously crunchy vegetable with a celery flavour. You will need to toss it in dressing soon after peeling to prevent the white flesh discolouring.

PREPARATION TIME: 20 mins

SERVES 4

METHOD

1 Peel the celeriac and grate finely.
2 Slice and core the apple, then cut it into thin slivers and mix it with the celeriac and nuts, reserving 2 or 3 slices for a garnish.
3 Mix soured cream or smetana, lemon juice and turmeric together, season to taste and add to the celeriac. Garnish with slices of apple.

FROM TOP: Creamed celeriac salad; Beetroot slaw with orange dressing; Red cabbage slaw with a sweet and sour dressing

RED CABBAGE SLAW WITH A SWEET AND SOUR DRESSING

INGREDIENTS

- 10oz (300g) red cabbage, finely shredded
- 4oz (125g) dried dates, stoned and chopped
- 1oz (25g) sunflower or pumpkin seeds

DRESSING

- 1 tbsp (15ml) sunflower oil
- 1 tbsp (15ml) lemon juice
- 1 tbsp (15ml) red wine vinegar
- 2 tsp (10ml) capers, finely chopped
- 1 tsp (5ml) wholegrain mustard
- 2 tsp (10ml) clear honey

Illustrated above

The strong flavour of red cabbage goes well with fruit, especially dates or raisins, and is enhanced by a sweet sauce and the nutty taste of sunflower or pumpkin seeds. Red cabbage is tougher than white and needs to be cut into very fine shreds.

PREPARATION TIME: 20 mins

SERVES 4

METHOD

1 Prepare the cabbage and dates. Mix with the pumpkin or sunflower seeds in a large bowl.
2 For the dressing, combine all the ingredients together. Season to taste.
3 Mix the dressing into the slaw and serve immediately.

FROM TOP: Chicory and grapefruit salad; Classic green salad

CHICORY AND GRAPEFRUIT SALAD

INGREDIENTS

■ 1 pink grapefruit
■ 8oz (250g) chicory, chopped
■ 1 avocado, peeled and cubed
■ 4oz (125g) bean sprouts

DRESSING

■ ¼ pint (150ml) natural yogurt
■ 2 tbsp (30ml) grapefruit juice
■ 1 tsp (5ml) sunflower oil

Illustrated left

The sweet taste of pink grapefruit and smoothness of the avodaco soften the sharpness of the chicory. The low-fat dressing enhances the salad and enriches the texture and taste. Use ordinary grapefruit if pink is unavailable, but add a little orange juice to the dressing for sweetness.

PREPARATION TIME: 30 mins

SERVES 4

METHOD

1 Halve the grapefruit. Cut the flesh of one half into small pieces and reserve the other half for the juice in the dressing.
2 Prepare the other salad ingredients and mix together.
3 For the dressing, mix all the ingredients in a blender or food processor until smooth.
4 Serve the salad with the dressing poured over the top.

CLASSIC GREEN SALAD

INGREDIENTS

■ 1 small lettuce heart
■ 1 small crisp lettuce
■ ¼ cucumber, sliced
■ 4 spring onions
■ 1 small bunch watercress
■ 4–5 sprigs fresh lovage
■ 1 tbsp (15ml) olive oil

DRESSING

■ 1–2 tbsp (15-30ml) lemon juice
■ large pinch mustard powder
■ ¼ tsp celery seeds
■ 1 tsp (5ml) concentrated apple juice or clear honey
■ 1 clove garlic, crushed
■ black pepper

Illustrated above

Simple and inexpensive, a classic green salad with a variety of salad leaves and a good dressing makes a refreshing accompaniment to any dish. For variety you could use frisé, oakleaf lettuce or lamb's lettuce.

PREPARATION TIME: 30 mins

SERVES 4

METHOD

1 Select the best salad leaves, prepare them carefully, place in a large bowl and refrigerate.
2 Prepare the other salad ingredients and add to the salad leaves in the fridge.
3 Just before serving, toss the salad in the olive oil.
4 For the dressing, mix the remaining ingredients together and toss into the salad.
5 Serve immediately.

TOMATO AND ORANGE SALAD WITH NUTMEG DRESSING

INGREDIENTS

■ 4 tomatoes
■ 2 oranges
■ 8oz (250g) broccoli
■ 4oz (125g) turnip

DRESSING

■ juice and rind of ½ an orange
■ 1 tbsp (15ml) white wine vinegar
■ 1 tbsp (15ml) sunflower oil
■ ¼ tsp grated nutmeg
■ salt and pepper

Illustrated right

In this colourful salad the turnip and broccoli create a solid base for the vitamin C-rich oranges and tomatoes. A hint of spice in the dressing lends an added tang to the pervading orange flavour.

PREPARATION TIME: 15 mins

SERVES 4

METHOD

1 Slice the tomatoes. Peel and segment the oranges. Wash and trim the broccoli. Scrub, then chop the turnip.
2 For the dressing, mix the ingredients and season to taste.
3 Toss the dressing into the salad and serve immediately.

CALIFORNIAN SALAD WITH TARRAGON DRESSING

INGREDIENTS

- 2 large peaches
- 6 radishes
- 1oz (25g) hazelnuts
- 4oz (125g) green beans, trimmed
- ½ punnet salad cress

DRESSING

- 1 tbsp (15ml) olive oil
- 1 tbsp (15ml) white wine vinegar
- 1 tsp (5ml) honey
- 1 tsp (5ml) soya sauce
- 2 tsp (10ml) fresh tarragon

Illustrated right

Crunchy nuts, soft fruits and crisp vegetables create a wonderful combination of textures, flavours and nutrients. If you do not have the suggested combinations of root and shoot vegetables and fruits, try improvising with alternatives.

PREPARATION TIME: 20 mins

SERVES 4

METHOD

1 Cut the peaches and radishes into thin slices.

2 Lightly toast the hazelnuts under a preheated grill for 2-3 minutes to bring out the flavour. Then slice.

3 Chop the beans into 1-inch (2.5cm) lengths. Cut the cress.

4 Mix all the salad ingredients together in a large bowl.

5 For the dressing, thoroughly mix the ingredients and pour over the salad.

FRUIT AND FENNEL SALAD

INGREDIENTS

- 8oz (250g) seedless green grapes
- 12oz (375g) fennel, trimmed and chopped
- 2oz (50g) blanched almonds, halved
- 4oz (125g) radicchio

DRESSING

- ¼ pint (150ml) natural yogurt
- 1–2 tsp (5–10ml) creamed horseradish
- ¼ tsp turmeric or saffron infused in a little water

Illustrated right

The dry, crisp taste of almonds combines well with the clean, aniseed taste of fennel and the sweetness of the grapes. The low-calorie dressing has a similar blend of piquant and refreshing flavours.

PREPARATION TIME: 25 mins

SERVES 4

METHOD

1 Place the salad ingredients in a serving bowl.

2 Mix together the yogurt, horseradish and spices.

3 Toss the salad in the dressing.

FROM TOP: Tomato and orange salad with nutmeg dressing; Californian salad with tarragon dressing; Fruit and fennel salad

LOW-CALORIE MAYONNAISE

INGREDIENTS

- ¼ pint (150ml) Light Mayonnaise or reduced calorie mayonnaise
- ¼ pint natural yogurt
- ½ red pepper
- 1 tsp (5ml) paprika
- salt and pepper

Illustrated right

This low-fat mayonnaise, made half of mayonnaise and half of yogurt, is enriched by the added spice and red pepper and makes a good creamy dressing on any salad.

PREPARATION TIME: 10 mins (plus 15 mins if making mayonnaise)
MAKES ½ pint (300ml)

METHOD

1 Mix together mayonnaise and yogurt.
2 Deseed the red pepper and dice finely.
3 Add the pepper and paprika to the dressing.
4 Season to taste.

AIOLI

INGREDIENTS

- 1 egg
- 1–2 tbsp (15–30ml) lemon juice or white wine vinegar
- 3–4 cloves garlic
- ½ pint (300ml) mixed olive and sunflower oil
- pinch mustard powder
- salt and pepper
- 1 tbsp (15ml) boiling water

Illustrated right

This classic garlic mayonnaise from France is based on the Light Mayonnaise (see p.109), but for a richer, darker dressing you could use the Classic Mayonnaise and add the garlic before dripping in the oil.

PREPARATION TIME: 20 mins
MAKES ½ pint (300ml)

METHOD

1 In a food processor or blender, beat the egg thoroughly with the lemon juice or vinegar.
2 Crush the cloves of garlic and stir into the egg mixture.
3 Add the oil very gradually, beating continuously.
4 When smooth, add the mustard powder and season to taste.
5 Beat in the boiling water to stabilize the mayonnaise.

CLOCKWISE FROM TOP LEFT: Low-calorie mayonnaise; Aioli; Herb mayonnaise; Curried mayonnaise; Classic mayonnaise; Light mayonnaise

LIGHT MAYONNAISE

INGREDIENTS

- 1 egg
- 1–2 tbsp (15–30ml) lemon juice or white wine vinegar
- ½ pint (300ml) mixed olive and sunflower oil
- pinch mustard powder
- salt and pepper
- 1 tbsp (15ml) boiling water

Illustrated left

This lighter version of Classic Mayonnaise uses only one egg, which helps to keep the calorie and cholesterol levels down. Since the mixture is also less likely to curdle, it is easy to make in a blender or food processor. The egg white will help to thicken the mixture.

PREPARATION TIME: 15 mins
MAKES ½ pint (300ml)

METHOD

1 Using a whisk or blender, beat the egg thoroughly with the lemon juice or vinegar.
2 Add the oil very gradually, beating continuously.
3 When smooth, add the mustard powder and season to taste.
4 Beat in the boiling water to stabilize the mayonnaise.

HERB MAYONNAISE

INGREDIENTS

- 1 egg
- 1–2 tbsp (15–30ml) lemon juice or white wine vinegar
- 5–5 tbsp (75–90ml) chopped fresh tarragon
- ½ pint (300ml) mixed olive and sunflower oil
- pinch mustard powder
- salt and pepper
- 1 tbsp (15ml) boiling water

Illustrated left

If you prefer the rich Classic Mayonnaise to the light version, use two eggs instead of one. Parsley and chives also work well with mayonnaise.

PREPARATION TIME: 20 mins
MAKES ½ pint (300ml)

METHOD

1 Beat the egg thoroughly with the lemon juice or vinegar.
2 Stir in the chopped herbs.
3 Add the oil very slowly, beating continuously.
4 When smooth, add the mustard powder and season to taste.
5 Beat in the boiling water to stabilize the mayonnaise.

CLASSIC MAYONNAISE

INGREDIENTS

- 2 egg yolks
- ½ pint (300ml) mixed olive and sunflower oil
- 1–2 tbsp (15–30ml) lemon juice or white wine vinegar
- pinch mustard powder
- salt and pepper
- 1 tbsp (15ml) boiling water

Illustrated left

A classic mayonnaise can be used as a base for other salad dressings, as part of a recipe, or simply as a rich dressing in its own right. It is high in fat, so use sparingly, or mix with natural yogurt or fromage frais. It will keep for at least a week in a cool place.

PREPARATION TIME: 15 mins (plus chilling time)
MAKES ½ pint (300ml)

METHOD

1 Beat the egg yolks thoroughly, in a blender or with a whisk.
2 Add half the oil, a drip at a time, beating continuously.
3 Add 1 tbsp (15ml) lemon juice or vinegar and the mustard powder. Beat well.
4 Add the remaining oil; a tablespoon at a time if whisking by hand; in a steady stream if using an electric whisk. Season.
5 Beat in the boiling water, to stabilize the mayonnaise. Refrigerate and serve chilled.

CURRIED MAYONNAISE

INGREDIENTS

- 1 quantity of Classic or Light Mayonnaise
- 1 small Spanish onion
- 2oz (50g) dried apricots
- 2 tbsp (30ml) clear honey
- ½ tsp turmeric
- pinch chilli powder
- ½ tsp cumin seeds
- ½ tsp chopped fresh coriander leaves
- salt and pepper

Illustrated left

This spicy mayonnaise can be used as a rich dressing, dip or sauce. The added ingredients contribute additional vitamins and minerals without significantly adding to the calories. If you are anxious to reduce calories, however, use the lighter version as a base.

PREPARATION TIME: 30 mins
MAKES ½ pint (300ml)

METHOD

1 Make up the mayonnaise, using the light or classic method.
2 Peel the onion and dice finely.
3 Cut the dried apricots into small pieces.
4 Mix the onion, apricots, honey and spices into the mayonnaise.
5 Season to taste.

HERBS

*H*erbs should enhance and reinforce the character of a dish, not overpower it. They should usually be kept fresh, though oregano, dill, sage, marjoram and bay leaf keep well. To dry herbs, pick before flowering and hang upside down somewhere cool and dark. When dry, crumble and store in airtight containers.

BAY LEAF

This is the leaf of the Mediterranean sweet bay tree and an ingredient of bouquet garni. Used as a single leaf, it must be removed before serving.

DILL WEED

A subtly aromatic taste, well-suited to mild foods such as potatoes.

DILL SEEDS

More pungent than dill weed, they combine well with starchy foods, also enhancing their flavour.

OREGANO

The wild form of marjoram, very popular in Italy, especially with tomatoes, cheese and beans.

ROSEMARY

A strong, aromatic herb with a camphor-like smell. Its flavour goes well with rich, starchy foods and adds a piquancy to sauces.

THYME

A popular herb used in bouquet garnis and most vegetable dishes. It has an essential oil, thymol, thought to aid the digestion of fatty foods.

BASIL

Fresh, this herb tastes something like cloves; dried, it is like curry.

MARJORAM

A fragrant herb, both dried and fresh.

CONTINENTAL PARSLEY

This parsley is said to have a finer taste than English parsley. Both have Vitamin C and iron.

ENGLISH PARSLEY

One of the herbs in a bouquet garni, parsley is also used as a garnish and in sauces and stuffings.

APPLE MINT

This and spearmint are the best mints to use in sweet or savoury cooking.

CHERVIL

Best used fresh and added just before serving as cooking diminishes the taste. Ideal with finely textured food.

TARRAGON

A distinctly aromatic herb, often used in soups and salads. The French variety is superior to others.

SAGE

An excellent herb to counter richness, although it can be overpowering. Use to flavour bean or pea casseroles.

CHIVES

Subtler tasting and more digestible than onions, they lose their taste when dried, unless freeze-dried. Add to food at the end of cooking.

111

SPICES

*S*pices are indispensible to good cooking, providing infinitely varied flavours and vitamins and minerals. Buy spices whole and grate or grind them as required; once ground they should be stored in airtight containers.

CLOVES

The strong-tasting buds of a species of myrtle tree, cloves are usually used whole, but the heads can be ground for a more diluted spice.

BLUE POPPY
SEEDS

A mild spice, usually used to decorate or fill bread and confectionery, but also to spice rice dishes.

MUSTARD SEEDS

Black seeds are the strongest; the white are used as a spice, as the basis for commercial mustards and as a flavouring, for example in pickles.

CARAWAY
SEEDS

A pungent spice, native to Europe and Asia. Used to flavour soups, casseroles, vegetables and cheeses.

GROUND
CUMIN

This spice is popular in curries because of its pungent, slightly bitter taste.

CUMIN SEED

Used whole or ground, these seeds have a hot flavour.

CAYENNE PEPPER

The name covers a wide range of seeds from the capsicum family. Very pungent, so use sparingly in curries and casseroles.

CORIANDER

The seeds, whole or ground, are extensively used in curries, soups and stewed or baked fruits, and aid the digestion of starch.

JUNIPER
BERRIES

A pungent, slightly resinous spice, used to flavour gin and good with pasta and cabbage.

CINNAMON

Available either as strips of bark or as powder.

NUTMEG and MACE

Nutmeg is the sweet dried seed of a southeast Asian tree; mace is the savoury outer husk.

MIXED SPICE

A mix of any sweet spices available. Used in desserts.

CHILLI

Hotter than paprika, chilli is used extensively in curries and any dish in need of a bite.

TURMERIC

A slightly musty spice used in curries and pickles. The powder and the dried root of the plant are available.

PAPRIKA

This mildly hot, sweet spice comes from the ground seeds of pimiento, and is good with goulashes and sauces.

ANISEED

Also called sweet cumin, aniseed is a sweetly aromatic spice used in smooth soups and baking.

GARAM MASALA

The name means "hot mixture" and this can be bought or made from cinnamon, cloves, cumin seeds, cardamoms and mace.

ROOT GINGER

This excellent culinary spice, from the rhizome of an Asian plant, is rich in minerals and should be bought fresh.

ALLSPICE

The dried fruit of the pimento tree, used in savoury sauces, baking and pickling.

113

FLAVOURINGS

*I*n addition to traditional flavourings such as garlic and tomato purée there is a wide variety of healthy alternatives to salt and sugar, ranging from exotic ingredients such as soya sauce to old favourites like honey. As well as enhancing the flavour of any dish, they also provide valuable vitamins and minerals.

TABASCO

A hot relish made from peppers, vinegar and salt, from the Tabasco region of Mexico.

WHOLEGRAIN MUSTARD

A hot mustard made from whole white seeds, white wine, allspice and black pepper.

CAPERS

Capers are the unopened buds of a Mediterranean shrub which are pickled to enhance their slightly hot aniseed flavour.

GARLIC

An excellent flavouring for any savoury dish, garlic is usually associated with Mediterranean and Eastern countries.

TOMATO PURÉE

Indispensable in pizzas and most pasta dishes, this is a good source of Vitamins A, B$_2$ and C and of folic acid and potassium.

GREEN CHILLI PEPPERS

Green chillis ripen to red and both are very hot. The capsicin in them can burn the skin and eyes, so prepare them carefully and wash your hands afterwards.

YEAST EXTRACT

A rich source of B Vitamins that helps in the digestion of carbohydrates.

STUFFED GREEN OLIVES

These are unripe black olives stuffed with pimiento. Excellent garnishes, they are high in minerals.

SOYA SAUCE

A fermented soya bean product, high in B Vitamins

CLEAR HONEY

A good natural sweetener, with B Vitamins and traces of minerals.

PEANUT BUTTER

A healthy flavouring for dips, sauces and dressings, and full of protein, vitamins and minerals.

VEGETABLE ACCOMPANIMENTS

FRENCH BEANS AND SWEETCORN WITH MINT SAUCE	118
REFRITOS	118
BROAD BEANS WITH CREAMY BASIL SAUCE	118
CARROTS AND DILL	118
CELERY AND LEEKS IN SHERRY	119
MEDITERRANEAN POTATOES	119
RED CABBAGE AND APPLE	119

FROM TOP: French beans and sweetcorn with mint sauce (see p.118); Refritos (see p.118); Broad beans with creamy basil sauce (see p.118)

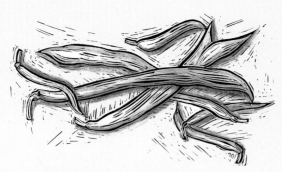

FRENCH BEANS AND SWEETCORN
■ WITH MINT SAUCE ■

INGREDIENTS

■ 1 head of sweetcorn (or 8oz/ 250g fresh or frozen sweetcorn kernels)
■ 8oz (250g) French beans, trimmed and chopped
SAUCE
■ ³⁄₄oz (20g) margarine
■ ½oz (15g) wholemeal flour
■ ½ pint (300ml) skimmed milk
■ 1 tbsp (15ml) fresh mint
■ 1 tbsp (15ml) white wine vinegar
■ salt and black pepper

Illustrated on page 117

This makes a colourful, high-protein side dish to accompany a bake or roast or boost the fibre content of a meal made from dairy products. The beans and corn are relatively low in fats and go very well with the creamy white sauce sharpened with a little vinegar.
PREPARATION TIME: 15 mins
COOKING TIME: 15 mins
SERVES 4

METHOD

1 If using a head of sweetcorn, boil in plenty of water for about 7 minutes, then slice the kernels off the cob.
2 Steam the French beans for 5 minutes or until just tender. Mix with the sweetcorn.
3 For the sauce, melt the margarine in a pan and sprinkle with the flour. Cook for 3 minutes. Gradually add the milk, stirring constantly, and bring the sauce to boiling point. Then add the mint and simmer for 5 minutes. Stir in the vinegar and season.
4 Pour on to the freshly cooked beans and corn. Serve immediately.

■ REFRITOS ■

INGREDIENTS

■ 2 tbsp (30ml) olive oil
■ 2 medium onions, peeled and chopped
■ 2 cloves garlic, crushed
■ 2 tsp (10ml) chopped fresh chillies
■ 1lb (500g) cooked red kidney beans
■ 4 tomatoes, skinned and sliced
■ 2 tsp (10ml) dried oregano
■ 1–2 tbsp (15–30ml) red wine vinegar
■ salt and pepper

Illustrated on page 117

This is a useful South American recipe for left-over beans.
PREPARATION TIME: 15 mins
COOKING TIME: 10–15 mins
SERVES 4

METHOD

1 Heat the oil in a pan and gently fry the onion until soft. Add the garlic and chillies and cook for 2 minutes.
2 Mash the kidney beans and place in the pan with the tomatoes and oregano.
3 Stir in the vinegar, season and cook the mixture for 10–15 minutes to heat through and allow the flavours to develop.

BROAD BEANS WITH
■ CREAMY BASIL SAUCE ■

INGREDIENTS

■ 1lb (500g) fresh or frozen broad beans
SAUCE
■ ³⁄₄oz (20g) margarine
■ ½oz (15g) wholemeal flour
■ ½ pint (300ml) skimmed milk
■ ½ tsp mustard powder
■ 2 tbsp (30ml) fresh basil
■ 2 tbsp (30ml) soured cream or smetana

Illustrated on page 117

Use this recipe to complement a grain dish such as rice or wheat or to boost the fibre content of a low-fibre dish such as an omelette.
PREPARATION TIME: 15 mins
COOKING TIME: 15 mins
SERVES 4

METHOD

1 Lightly steam the broad beans for 5–7 minutes or until just tender.
2 For the sauce melt the margarine in a pan. Stir in the flour and cook for 3 minutes. Gradually add milk, stirring constantly, and bring to boiling point. Then simmer, add the the mustard and basil and cook for a further 5 minutes, stirring constantly.
3 Cool slightly, then stir in the soured cream or smetana. Pour over the freshly cooked broad beans and serve.

■ CARROTS AND DILL ■

INGREDIENTS

■ 2 tsp (10ml) sunflower oil
■ 1 large onion, sliced into fine rings
■ 1lb (500g) carrots, cut into fingers
■ 1 tsp (5ml) dill seeds
■ ½ tsp yeast extract
■ ¼ pint (150ml) hot water
■ salt and black pepper

Illustrated right

The carrot is a nutritious vegetable. It contains a high concentration of carotene, which converts to Vitamin A in the body, and is richer in calcium and potassium than most other vegetables. Dill provides an exciting flavour that contrasts with sweet whole baby carrots, which are available in late spring and summer.
PREPARATION TIME: 20 mins
COOKING TIME: 10 mins
SERVES 4

METHOD

1 Heat the oil in a saucepan and fry the onion, carrots and dill for 5–10 minutes.
2 Dissolve the yeast extract in the hot water and pour over the carrots. Cover and cook gently for 10 minutes until the carrots are just tender, adding a little extra water if necessary. Season to taste and serve hot.

FROM LEFT: Carrots and dill; Celery and leeks in sherry; Mediterranean potatoes; Red cabbage and apple

MEDITERRANEAN POTATOES

INGREDIENTS

- ½ tsp olive oil
- 1½lb (750g) potatoes, cut into chunks
- 6 cloves garlic, chopped
- ¼ pint (150ml) red wine
- 1 tbsp (15ml) tomato purée
- 2½ fl oz (65ml) water
- 1 tsp (5ml) chopped fresh rosemary
- 1 tsp (5ml) chopped fresh oregano
- 2 tbsp (30ml) chopped fresh parsley
- ¼ tsp black pepper

Illustrated left

In this aromatic dish, the potatoes absorb the flavours of the herbs, garlic and red wine when they are cooked in the oven. If you prefer, replace the wine with 1 tbsp (15ml) red wine vinegar and ¼ pint (150ml) water.

PREPARATION TIME: 15 mins
COOKING TIME: 1¼ hours
SERVES 4

METHOD

1 Brush a large ovenproof dish or casserole with the olive oil. Put in the potatoes and garlic.
2 Mix together the red wine, tomato purée, water, rosemary, oregano, parsley and pepper. Pour over the potatoes.
3 Cover and bake in a preheated oven at Gas Mark 5, 375°F, 190°C for 1¼ hours, or until the potatoes are tender. Serve hot.

CELERY AND LEEKS IN SHERRY

INGREDIENTS

- ¼ tsp olive oil
- 6 sticks celery, cut into 1 inch (2.5cm) slices
- 12oz (375g) leeks, cut into 1 inch (2.5cm) slices
- ¼ pint (150ml) medium sherry
- ¼ tsp black pepper
- 1 tsp chopped fresh thyme
- 1 tbsp (15ml) apple juice

Illustrated above

This quickly prepared dish combines two vegetables that are both low in calories and high in fibre. The stock from the cooked celery and leeks could be drained off, and thickened with a little cornflour or arrowroot to make a delicious sauce. Serve this as a side dish or as a hot starter with garlic bread.

PREPARATION TIME: 10 mins
COOKING TIME: 1¼ hours
SERVES 4

METHOD

1 Brush the oil around the inside of a casserole or ovenproof dish. Layer the celery and leeks in the casserole.
2 Mix together the sherry, pepper, thyme and apple juice. Pour over the celery and leeks. Cover the casserole.
3 Bake in a preheated oven at Gas Mark 5, 375°F, 190°C for 1¼ hours or until the vegetables are tender. Serve hot.

RED CABBAGE AND APPLE

INGREDIENTS

- 1¼lb (625g) red cabbage, sliced
- 6oz (175g) pickling onions or shallots, cut in half
- 1 large clove garlic, chopped
- 12oz (375g) eating apples, cored and sliced
- 1 tsp (5ml) dill seeds
- 2 cloves
- 1oz (25g) sultanas
- 2 fl oz (50ml) cider vinegar
- 3 fl oz (75ml) water
- 2 tbsp (30ml) apple juice

Illustrated left

This traditional recipe is made slightly more unusual by the addition of sultanas and cloves. It is easy to prepare and with its slightly piquant flavour makes a good accompaniment to richer dishes like a loaf or a roast.

PREPARATION TIME: 10 mins
COOKING TIME: 1¼ hours
SERVES 4

METHOD

1 Layer the cabbage, onion, garlic, apple, dill seeds, cloves and sultanas in a large casserole.
2 Mix together the cider vinegar, water and apple juice. Pour over the vegetables. Cover the casserole.
3 Bake in a preheated oven at Gas Mark 4, 350°F, 180°C for 1¼ hours. Serve this dish hot or cold.

SEEDS, NUTS AND DRIED FRUIT

*S*eeds and nuts are a good source of protein, vitamins and minerals, while dried fruits contain concentrated amounts of iron and other minerals, B and C Vitamins and sugar. Dried fruit will keep for over 6 months in an airtight container. Shelled nuts should be stored in a cool, dry place and used as soon as possible. Unshelled and unsalted nuts keep longer.

PRUNES

These dried black plums are low in calories, but high in potassium and fibre, and the tenderized variety can be cooked in 8 minutes. Prunes are sold with or without stones.

GROUND ALMONDS

When ground, these high-protein, low-fat nuts can be used to replace some of the flour in cakes and savoury dishes.

PISTACHIOS

Bright green pistachio nuts are usually sold in their shells. To preserve the natural colour, shell, boil and skin the nuts.

SUNFLOWER SEEDS

An excellent source of E and most B Vitamins, especially B_1, and essential fatty acids, sunflower seeds are also rich in iron and are used in bakes and garnishes.

BRAZIL NUTS

Brazils are rich in protein, fibre, magnesium, zinc, calcium, phosphorus, E and B Vitamins, and have the highest fat level of any nut.

DRIED DATES

High in Vitamin A and niaicin, dried dessert dates are sold unstoned, while cooking dates are sold stoned in blocks.

SULTANAS

These dried grapes are larger and sweeter than raisins and equally high in Vitamin B_6 and potassium.

PINE KERNELS

The seeds of the Mediterranean stone pine tree are roasted and make a good snack or topping for salads.

CASHEW NUTS

Although high in calories and fat, cashews are full of valuable vitamins and minerals. The healthiest types are roasted and unsalted.

ALMONDS

Sweet almonds contain more protein than any other nut and can be served whole, crushed or ground into a paste. Bitter almonds are distilled into almond essence.

HAZELNUTS

Lower in fat than most other nuts, rich in Vitamin E, and a good source of protein, this nut is good toasted, in stuffings, salads and roasts.

PEANUTS

Peanuts are legumes but they are eaten as nuts. They are very high in protein and contain E and B Vitamins, iron, zinc and potassium.

DRIED APRICOTS

Dried apricots are extremely high in protein, fibre, and Vitamins A and C. Try to avoid those preserved in sugar.

SESAME SEEDS

One of the oldest spices and oil-seed crops, these seeds are also made into tahini and gomashio (a salt substitute) and make an excellent garnish. High in calcium, phosphorus and zinc.

WALNUTS

High in fat and a good source of protein, fibre, vitamins and minerals, walnuts are generally used in sweet recipes, although they are also excellent in salads, stuffings, and roasts.

FRESH COCONUT

To check that a coconut is fresh, shake it to hear the milk. Use in curries, rice dishes and desserts.

DRIED FIGS

Iron-rich and high in fibre, dried figs are also high in sugar, so avoid those with an added dusting of sugar.

PUDDINGS

KIWI AND PASSION FRUIT CAKE	124
PANCAKE BATTER FLAN WITH PEARS AND RED PLUMS	125
WHOLEMEAL BANANA PANCAKES	125
FRUIT PANCAKE GATEAU	125
FRUIT RISOTTO	126
BANANA SURPRISE	126
GOLDEN FRUIT SALAD	126
MELON AND STRAWBERRY SALAD WITH CREAMY ORANGE TOPPING	127
FILLED MELON SALAD	127
MIXED FRUIT SALAD IN SPICED YOGURT	128
FRESH DATE AND MANGO PLATTER	128
LATE SUMMER SALAD	129
STUFFED KIWI FRUIT	129
TROPICAL SALAD	130
COTTAGE CHEESE AND FRUIT PLATTER	130
FRUIT AND NUT SALAD	130
MIXED FRUIT BOWL WITH CHEESE PLATTER AND NUTS	131
SPICED FRUIT COMPOTE	131
MAKING REDCURRANT SAUCE	132
POACHED PEARS WITH REDCURRANT SAUCE	132
SPICED PUREE WITH FRESH APPLE	132
STRAWBERRY CHEESECAKE	133
PAWPAW AND LYCHEE PAVLOVA	134
MAKING A PAVLOVA	134
SUMMER PUDDING	135
ORANGE AND RAISIN GRANOLA	135
PEAR AND ALMOND PUDDING	135
PLUM CHARLOTTE	136
PINEAPPLE PUDDING	137
APRICOT AND GOOSEBERRY FLAN	137
ORANGE AND APPLE FLAN	138
MAKING PANCAKE CUSHIONS	138
PEACH AND NUTMEG CUSHIONS	139
CHEESE PANCAKES WITH APPLE SAUCE	140
CHERRY OATEN PANCAKES	140
SAUCER PANCAKES	141
LEMON AND BANANA ROULADE	141
WATERMELON SORBET	142
GREEN GRAPE SORBET	142
AUTUMN FRUIT SALAD	142
HAZELNUT AND RASPBERRY DESSERT	143
PINEAPPLE BASKET	143

Kiwi and passion fruit cake (see p.124)

KIWI AND PASSION FRUIT CAKE

INGREDIENTS

BASE

- 3oz (75g) margarine
- 2oz (50g) soft brown sugar
- 1½oz (40g) wholemeal breadcrumbs
- 1oz (25g) rolled oats
- 2oz (50g) wholemeal flour
- 1½oz (40g) ground almonds
- ¼ tsp almond essence

TOPPING

- 8oz (250g) ricotta cheese
- 8oz (250g) cream cheese
- 1oz (25g) soft brown sugar, or to taste
- 2 passion fruit
- 1 kiwi fruit, peeled and sliced

Illustrated on page 123

The crisp, crumbly, low-fat base of this dish complements the smooth texture of the ricotta and cream cheese topping and the slightly sharp fruit flavours. Sweet, juicy kiwi fruit slices make an attractive decoration. Kiwi fruit originally came from China, and are also known as Chinese gooseberries. They are now grown chiefly in New Zealand. They store well in a cool place and can be frozen successfully. You can eat the skin as well as the seeds and flesh, but they are usually peeled. The delicate flavour and colour of the kiwi fruit are complemented by the fragrance of the passion fruit. Choose the large, dark, crinkled passion fruit when buying. Cream cheese and ricotta cheese make a rich combination for the topping.

PREPARATION TIME: 35 mins (plus overnight standing time)
COOKING TIME: 15–20 mins
SERVES 4

METHOD

1 For the base, cream the butter and margarine together, add the remaining ingredients, and press into a loose-based 6-inch (15cm) flan tin.
2 Bake in a preheated oven at Gas Mark 5, 375°F, 190°C for 15–20 minutes. Leave the base to cool.
3 For the topping, beat the ricotta cheese, cream cheese, and sugar together in a blender. Spoon on to the base and leave to set overnight.
4 Scoop out the flesh of the passion fruit and spread it evenly over the top of the cheesecake. Decorate the cake with the slices of kiwi fruit.

FROM TOP: Fruit pancake gateau; Pancake batter flan with pears and red plums; Wholemeal banana pancakes

PANCAKE BATTER FLAN WITH PEARS AND RED PLUMS

INGREDIENTS

- 1 egg
- ¼ pint (150ml) skimmed milk
- 1 tbsp (15ml) honey
- 3oz (75g) wholemeal flour
- 8oz (250g) pears, cored and thickly sliced
- 8oz (250g) red plums, stoned and thickly sliced

Illustrated left

Use ripe, sweet dessert pears if you can.

PREPARATION TIME: 10 mins
COOKING TIME: 40 mins
SERVES 4–6

METHOD

1 For the batter, put the egg, milk and honey into a blender or food processor and liquidize for 30 seconds. Add the flour and liquidize for a further 30 seconds.
2 Grease a 10-inch (25cm) fluted flan dish. Pour the batter in and put the pears and plums on top, letting them sink in slightly.
3 Bake in a preheated oven at Gas Mark 6, 400°F, 200°C for 40 minutes until the fruit is soft and the flan is brown on top.

WHOLEMEAL BANANA PANCAKES

INGREDIENTS

- 1 tsp (5ml) arrowroot or cornflour
- ¼ pint (150ml) water
- 12oz (375g) black cherries, stoned
- 1 tbsp (15ml) honey
- 1 egg yolk
- 2 ripe bananas, mashed
- ¼ pint (150ml) skimmed milk
- 4oz (125g) wholemeal flour
- ¼ tsp sunflower oil
- 5 fl oz (150ml) natural yogurt
- 1 tsp (5ml) clear honey

Illustrated left

The bananas help to make these pancakes moist as well as sweet.

PREPARATION TIME: 10 mins
COOKING TIME: 20 mins
MAKES: 16 small pancakes

METHOD

1 For the sauce, put the arrowroot or cornflour in a saucepan and mix to a smooth paste with 1 tsp (5ml) water. Add the remaining water, black cherries and honey and boil. Reduce the heat and simmer for 5 minutes.
2 For the batter, liquidize the egg yolk, mashed bananas and milk for 30 seconds. Add the flour and liquidize for 30 seconds.
3 Grease a hot griddle or heavy-based frying pan. Use about 1 tbsp (15ml) pancake batter for each pancake. Cook until bubbles break on the surface and begin to set. Turn and cook for a further 1–2 minutes. Mix the yogurt with the honey. Serve the pancakes with the cherry sauce poured over them, and the yogurt and honey spooned on top.

FRUIT PANCAKE GATEAU

INGREDIENTS

- 1 quantity of wholemeal batter (see p.80)
- 8oz (250g) strawberries
- 1 tsp (5ml) arrowroot or cornflour
- 2 peaches, peeled and thinly sliced
- 6oz (175g) peeled pineapple, roughly chopped
- 3oz (75g) creamed coconut, grated
- ¼ pint (150ml) hot water

Illustrated left

Fresh-tasting strawberries, peaches and pineapple combine here to make a delicious summer dessert. This recipe only requires four pancakes, but the batter is enough to make at least eight. The remaining pancakes can be frozen for later use.

PREPARATION TIME: 30 mins (plus 30 mins for the batter)
COOKING TIME: 30 mins plus 15 mins for the pancakes
MAKES: 8 pancakes

METHOD

1 Make the pancakes (see p.80). Pile the cooked pancakes on a plate and cover to keep warm.
2 For the filling, put the strawberries in a saucepan, reserving some for decoration. Sprinkle over the arrowroot or cornflour and stir over a medium heat until a thick purée is formed. Remove from the heat.
3 Grease a 7-inch (18cm) spring mould. Put 1 pancake in the bottom of the mould. Put a layer of sliced peaches on top of this, reserving some for garnish.
4 Put another pancake on top of the layer of peaches. Cover with all of the strawberry purée.
5 Cover the strawberries with another pancake and put the pineapple on top.
6 Cover the pineapple with another pancake and finish with a layer of peaches.
7 Cover the spring mould with foil and bake in a preheated oven at Gas Mark 4, 350°F, 180°C for 30 minutes.
8 Meanwhile, for the coconut sauce, put the creamed coconut into a blender or food processor with the hot water and liquidize until smooth. Allow to cool and then pour into a small serving bowl.
9 When cooked, remove the gâteau from the spring mould and serve with the bowl of coconut cream and fresh strawberries.

FROM TOP: *Banana surprise; Fruit risotto*

■ FRUIT RISOTTO ■

INGREDIENTS

■ 8oz (250g) long-grain brown rice
■ 1 pint (600ml) skimmed milk
■ 1 tbsp (15ml) clear honey
■ 4oz (125g) black grapes, deseeded
■ 1 peach, pear or nectarine, sliced
■ 1 dessert apple, cored and sliced
■ 1 banana, sliced
■ 1 orange, cut into segments
■ 4oz (125g) melon or pineapple, cubed
■ 1oz (25g) flaked almonds, toasted
■ ½ tsp ground cinnamon

GARNISH

■ Greek yogurt
■ slices of orange

Illustrated above

This recipe makes a substantial dessert, sweetened only by the fruits and honey. Various fruits could be used with the rice according to availability. Serve topped with a little Greek yogurt and garnished with slices of orange.
PREPARATION TIME: 10 mins (plus cooling time)
COOKING TIME: 40 mins
SERVES 4

METHOD

1 Put the rice, milk and honey into a large pan. Bring to the boil, cover and simmer gently for 30–40 minutes.
2 Remove from the heat and stir in the grapes, peach, pear or nectarine, apple, banana, orange and melon or pineapple. Set aside to cool.
3 When cool, put the risotto into one large or four individual dishes. Sprinkle with flaked almonds and the cinnamon.

■ BANANA SURPRISE ■

INGREDIENTS

■ 4 medium bananas
■ 4 tbsp (60ml) fresh lemon juice
■ 2oz (50g) flaked almonds
■ ½ pint (300ml) natural yogurt
■ 1 tbsp (15ml) clear honey

GARNISH

■ lemon slices

Illustrated left

Baked bananas are surprisingly sweet and taste delicious with this yogurt topping.
PREPARATION TIME: 20 mins
COOKING TIME: 20 mins
SERVES 4

METHOD

1 Peel the bananas and slice into 1 inch (2.5cm) chunks. Put into a casserole or ovenproof dish and pour over the lemon juice.
2 Toast the almonds lightly under a preheated moderate grill for 5–10 minutes. Add to the banana. Cover and bake in a preheated oven at Gas Mark 4, 350°F, 180°C for 15 minutes.
3 Meanwhile, mix the yogurt with the honey.
4 Pour the yogurt over the bananas. Serve straightaway garnished with lemon slices.

■ GOLDEN FRUIT SALAD ■

INGREDIENTS

■ 12oz (375g) watermelon
■ 1 pomegranate
■ 8oz (250g) fresh pineapple
■ 2 nectarines

Illustrated right

There is sometimes no need to add extra liquid or sugar to a fruit salad, since most fruits provide plenty of natural juice. For balance, choose some watery ingredients such as melon for the liquid, and some sweet fruits such as nectarines for the flavour.
PREPARATION TIME: 20 mins (plus chilling time)
SERVES 4–6

METHOD

1 Remove the peel and the seeds from the watermelon and chop the flesh into medium chunks.
2 Slice the pomegranate in half and remove all the seeds, taking care not to put any yellow pith into the salad.
3 Cut the pineapple flesh into chunks. Stone and slice the nectarines.
4 Mix all the fruit carefully together in a serving bowl and refrigerate. Serve chilled.

MELON AND STRAWBERRY SALAD WITH CREAMY ORANGE TOPPING

INGREDIENTS

- 1lb (500g) Galia melon
- 8oz (250g) strawberries, hulled
- 7oz (200g) skimmed milk soft cheese (quark)
- juice of 1 large orange
- 2–3 drops of vanilla essence

Illustrated left

Skimmed milk soft cheese makes a delicious, high-protein topping to fruit and can be flavoured with any kind of fruit juice. Melon and strawberries make a wonderful, sweet combination, but if they are out of season, try improvising with other fruit.

PREPARATION TIME: 25 mins
SERVES 4

METHOD

1 Scoop the melon flesh into small balls with a spoon.
2 Slice the strawberries and mix with the melon balls. Refrigerate to chill.
3 In a blender, mix the quark with the orange juice and vanilla until smooth.
4 Serve the fruit salad with a topping of the quark mixture.

FILLED MELON SALAD

INGREDIENTS

- 2 Ogen melons
- 1 orange
- 6oz (175g) raspberries
- juice of 1 lime

Illustrated left

This attractive dessert of fruit-filled melon halves makes a light and clean-tasting end to a meal. Small Ogen melons from Israel have richly flavoured green flesh, which combines well with the sweet raspberry and orange flavours. Adding lime juice not only increases the vitamin content but also adds a refreshing tang.

PREPARATION TIME: 15 mins (plus chilling time
SERVES 4

METHOD

1 Cut the melons in half and discard the seeds. Scoop out a little of the flesh from the centre of each half.
2 Peel and segment the orange, reserving all the juice. Cut the segments in half.
3 Divide the raspberries and orange pieces between the melon halves, then sprinkle with a little lime juice. Refrigerate and serve chilled.

FROM TOP: Golden fruit salad; Melon and strawberry salad with creamy orange topping; Filled melon salad

MIXED FRUIT SALAD IN SPICED YOGURT

INGREDIENTS

- 4oz (125g) black grapes
- 2 large bananas
- 1 peach
- 1 crisp green apple
- 7–8 fl oz (200–250ml) natural yogurt
- 2–3 tbsp (30–45ml) soured cream or smetana (optional)
- ½ inch (1cm) freshly grated root ginger

GARNISH
- ground cinnamon

Illustrated right

Yogurt is a wonderful ingredient — it is low in fat, its live enzymes ward off harmful bacteria in the digestive system and it makes a useful substitute for cream. Here, the yogurt coating helps to preserve some of the more delicate vitamins that are destroyed when cut fruit is left exposed to the air.

PREPARATION TIME: 15 mins
SERVES 4

METHOD

1 Halve and deseed the grapes.
2 Peel and chop the bananas. Stone and chop the peach. Core and chop the apple.
3 Mix all the fruit with the natural yogurt, soured cream or smetana (if used) and ginger in a serving bowl. Sprinkle with cinnamon just before serving.

FRESH DATE AND MANGO PLATTER

INGREDIENTS

- 8–10oz (250–300g) fresh dates
- 1 large mango or 2 small mangoes
- 1oz (25g) slivered almonds
- 1oz (25g) cashew nut pieces

Illustrated right

Mangoes contain an enzyme that aids digestion, and when combined with dates and nuts provide a good balance of vitamins and minerals. Choose mangoes that smell ripe and are fairly soft to touch, and handle them gently.

PREPARATION TIME: 10 mins
COOKING TIME: 7–10 mins
SERVES 4

METHOD

1 Halve and stone the dates.
2 Peel the mango and slice the flesh coarsely, away from the stone. There should be about 1 lb (500g) of flesh.
3 Lightly toast the nuts under a preheated grill for 2–3 minutes, or in a preheated moderate oven at Gas Mark 4, 350°F, 180°C for 7–10 minutes.
4 Arrange the mango and dates on 4 individual plates, and sprinkle with toasted nuts.

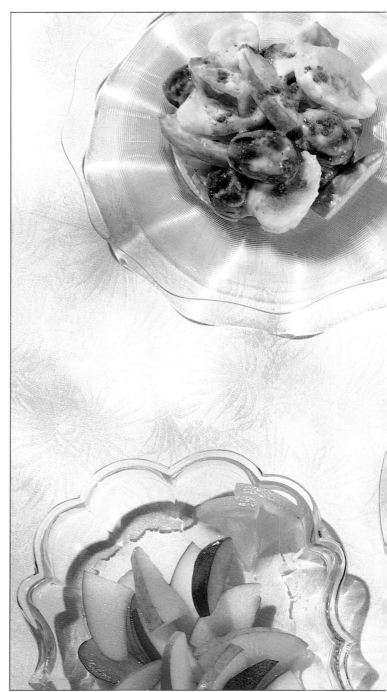

CLOCKWISE FROM TOP LEFT: Mixed fruit salad in spiced yogurt; Stuffed kiwi fruit; Fresh date and mango platter; Late summer salad

LATE SUMMER SALAD

INGREDIENTS

- 1 William pear
- 1 crisp red dessert apple
- 8oz (250g) red plums
- 8oz (250g) greengages
- ¼ pint (150ml) apple or pear juice

GARNISH
- 1 orange, thinly sliced

Illustrated left

Fruit salads can, of course, be made at any time of the year, but those made with late summer orchard fruit make a pleasant and inexpensive change from tropical versions.

PREPARATION TIME: 15 mins (plus chilling time)

SERVES 4

METHOD

1 Wash the fruit but do not peel.
2 Core and chop the pear and apple into chunky pieces. Stone and chop the plums and greengages.
3 Mix the fruits together with the fruit juice in a serving bowl. Garnish with the orange slices, refrigerate and serve chilled.

STUFFED KIWI FRUIT

INGREDIENTS

- 4 kiwi fruit
- 3oz (75g) cream cheese
- 1–2 tsp (5–10ml) chopped mint leaves
- 1oz (25g) soft brown sugar or honey, or to taste
- 4 large strawberries, hulled

GARNISH
- sprigs of fresh mint

Illustrated left

The kiwi fruit, a good source of Vitamin C, is often confined to garnishing. But filled with sweetened cream cheese and decorated with mint and strawberries, it makes a refreshing and nutritious dessert.

PREPARATION TIME: 25 mins

SERVES 4

METHOD

1 Slice a third off the top of each kiwi fruit, put to one side and prepare the remaining two thirds.
2 Scoop out the kiwi flesh, chop it or mash it, then mix with the cream cheese and mint. Sweeten with sugar or honey to taste.
3 Pile the cheese mixture back into the kiwi fruit.
4 Carefully peel the remaining pieces of kiwi fruit, cut into rings, then halve. Halve the strawberries.
5 Arrange the strawberry and kiwi slices on top of each stuffed kiwi fruit. Garnish with mint and serve on individual plates.

TROPICAL SALAD

INGREDIENTS

- 1 pawpaw
- 8oz (250g) fresh dates, stoned and halved
- 2 bananas, peeled and sliced
- juice of 1 lemon
- 2 tsp (10ml) clear honey
- 2 tbsp (30ml) grated creamed coconut

Illustrated right

This rich, silky fruit salad gains its velvety texture from the coconut as well as the smooth-fleshed fruits and honey. Pawpaw, or papaya, similar to a mango, is beneficial to the digestive system and is yellow when ripe. To ripen green fruit, leave in a warm place for a few days.

PREPARATION TIME: 20 mins

SERVES 4

METHOD

1 Halve the pawpaw, discarding the seeds. Peel and slice lengthwise.
2 Arrange the pawpaw, dates and bananas on serving plates, overlapping the slices.
3 Mix the lemon juice and honey together, then dribble over the fruit.
4 Top with the coconut.

COTTAGE CHEESE AND FRUIT PLATTER

INGREDIENTS

- 4oz (125g) green seedless grapes
- 2 passion fruit or 2 fresh figs, halved
- 4oz (125g) raspberries or redcurrants
- 4oz (125g) black cherries, blackberries or black grapes
- 1 orange
- 1 star fruit
- 8oz (250g) cottage cheese

GARNISH

- 4 walnut halves

Illustrated right

A beautiful way to present fruit, this dish is easy to prepare, provides a good balance of nutrients and can be made with any combination of exotic fruit. Star fruit has a delicate, sweet-sour flavour. It can be peeled, or not, as you prefer. To reduce the fat content use half-fat cottage cheese.

PREPARATION TIME: 20 mins

SERVES 4

METHOD

1 Wash all the fruit, string the redcurrants, peel and slice the orange and slice the star fruit.
2 Divide the cottage cheese and pile in the centre of 4 individual plates. Arrange the fruit in attractive clusters around the cheese. For example, 4 grapes in a bunch, half a passion fruit or fig, 3 raspberries, 2 slices of star fruit, 2 cherries, 4 more grapes, 2 slices of orange, 4 raspberries, 2 cherries.
3 Decorate the cheese with walnut halves.

FRUIT AND NUT SALAD

INGREDIENTS

- 1 peach, stoned and sliced
- 2 oranges, peeled and segmented
- 8oz (250g) fresh pineapple, peeled and chopped
- 6oz (175g) seedless green grapes
- 1oz (25g) Brazil nuts, chopped
- juice of 1 orange

Illustrated below

A small quantity of nuts adds protein and a new texture to a fruit salad. Nuts are best bought whole and then chopped, since broken pieces do not keep as well. To increase the protein content, try serving this dish with natural yogurt, soured cream or smetana.

PREPARATION TIME: 15 mins

SERVES 4

METHOD

1 Wash and prepare all the fruit. Arrange the slices of peach and orange in a circle on each serving plate.
2 Mix together the pineapple, grapes and nuts and pile into the middle of the circle.
3 Spoon over the orange juice.

FROM TOP: Cottage cheese and fruit platter; Tropical salad; Fruit and nut salad; Mixed fruit bowl with cheese platter and nuts

MIXED FRUIT BOWL WITH CHEESE PLATTER AND NUTS

INGREDIENTS

CHEESE
■ 3–4oz (75–125g) Camembert
■ 3–4oz (75-125g) curd cheese or Crowdie (finegrain cottage cheese)
■ 3–4oz (75–125g) Cheddar cheese

FRUIT AND NUTS
■ 2 apples
■ 2 nectarines
■ 2 oranges
■ 8oz (250g) fresh dates
■ 8oz (250g) black or green grapes
■ 8oz (250g) shelled mixed nuts

Illustrated left

The nuts can be served unshelled and the fruit left whole, if you prefer. Select them so that they provide plenty of contrast in shape and colour.

PREPARATION TIME: 10 mins
SERVES 8

METHOD

1 Put spoonfuls of soft cheeses and slices of the hard cheese around the outside of a large platter.
2 Slice the apples and nectarines, peel and segment the oranges, halve and stone the dates and deseed the grapes.
3 Arrange slices of the fruit in between the portions of cheese.
4 Place the nuts in small clusters in the centre of the platter.

SPICED FRUIT COMPOTE

INGREDIENTS

■ 8oz (250g) mixed dried fruit salad (such as prunes, apples, apricots, pears and peaches)
■ 6–8 cloves
■ 2-inch (5cm) cinnamon stick
■ ¼ tsp grated nutmeg

Illustrated right

Dried fruits are usually sun-dried to retain their natural sweetness, vitamins and minerals. To plump them up, rinse, then cover with liquid and leave to soak overnight. Use whole spices for flavouring, since the ground ones tend to discolour the fruit.

PREPARATION TIME: 5 mins (plus overnight soaking time)
COOKING TIME: 40–50 mins
SERVES 4

METHOD

1 Soak the fruit salad overnight in plenty of hot or cold water.
2 Place the fruit with the soaking liquid and spices in a saucepan. Bring to the boil, cover and simmer for 40–50 minutes.
3 Serve hot or cold.

FROM TOP: Poached pears with redcurrant sauce (see p.132); Spiced fruit compote; Spiced purée with fresh apple (see p.132)

MAKING REDCURRANT SAUCE

*R*edcurrants are an excellent source of fibre and Vitamin C and have always played an important role in traditional cooking – in jellies, jams and sauces. A versatile and healthy redcurrant sauce can be made without flour or sugar. It makes an excellent purée, which is worth sieving to make it smoother. If thick enough, it can be used as a sugar-free spread. The sauce will keep 3–4 days in the fridge.

1 Cook the redcurrants lightly in 2–3 tbsp (30–45ml) liquid for 3 minutes until the juices start to run.

2 Purée the cooked fruit mixture in a blender or food processor until smooth.

3 Sieve the sauce to remove the seeds and pith. If serving warm, heat gently.

POACHED PEARS WITH REDCURRANT SAUCE

INGREDIENTS

- 4 pears, peeled
- ½ pint (300ml) orange juice
- 1 tbsp (15ml) clear honey
- 1 bay leaf

SAUCE
- 8oz (250g) redcurrants

Illustrated on page 131

The delicate almond flavour of the bay leaf adds subtlety to the contrasting sweetness of the pears and the sharpness of the redcurrant sauce.

PREPARATION TIME: 30 mins (plus chilling time)

COOKING TIME: 20 mins

SERVES 4

METHOD

1 Place the pears in a pan with the orange juice, honey and bay leaf. Poach for 12–15 minutes, turning if necessary. Cool.
2 For the sauce, place the redcurrants with 2–3 tbsp (30–45ml) of the pear liquid in a saucepan and lightly cook for 3 minutes (see left).
3 Spoon some sauce on to each plate and stand a pear in the centre. Serve chilled.

SPICED PUREE WITH FRESH APPLE

INGREDIENTS

- 1lb (500g) cooking apples, peeled, cored and sliced
- 6 cloves
- juice of 1 orange
- ¾oz (20g) margarine
- ¼ pint (150ml) natural set yogurt

GARNISH
- 1 red crisp dessert apple, cored and sliced into very thin wedges

Illustrated on page 131

Fresh raw dessert apple adds a crisp dimension to the spicy cooking apple — and both are low in calories and fat-free. Natural set yogurt completes the balance of taste and nutrients in this simple recipe.

PREPARATION TIME: 15 mins

COOKING TIME: 10 mins

SERVES 4

METHOD

1 Place the cooking apples with the cloves and orange juice in a small pan.
2 Dot the margarine on top, and cover the apple mixture with greaseproof paper and a lid. Cook very gently for 10 minutes or until soft.
3 Purée in a blender or food processor, or sieve until smooth.
4 Place a few spoonfuls of purée in the centre of four individual plates. Spoon the yogurt around the outside.
5 Arrange the wedges of dessert apple on the top. Serve warm.

FROM TOP: Strawberry cheesecake; Pawpaw and lychee pavlova (see p.134); Summer pudding (see p.135)

STRAWBERRY CHEESECAKE

INGREDIENTS

BASE
- 2oz (50g) margarine
- 2 tbsp (30ml) soft brown sugar
- 1 egg yolk
- 2oz (50g) self-raising wholemeal flour

FILLING
- 8oz (250g) skimmed milk soft cheese (quark)
- 2 eggs
- ¼ pint (150ml) soured cream, smetana or natural yogurt

TOPPING
- 8oz (250g) strawberries

Illustrated left

This baked cheesecake, which sets when cooked, is made from a healthy mixture of low-fat soft cheese, eggs and soured cream or smetana. Uncooked versions often rely on double cream or full-fat cheese for texture. For an alternative healthy recipe that requires no cooking, use wholemeal digestive biscuits and margarine for the base, and mix honey with curd cheese and yogurt for the filling. Chill in the fridge for an hour and decorate with fresh summer fruit.

PREPARATION TIME: 45 mins
COOKING TIME: 45 mins
SERVES 6—8

METHOD

1 For the base, cream together the margarine and sugar in a bowl. Beat in the egg yolk and flour. Spread into a greased 7-inch (18cm) loose-based cake tin.

2 Bake in a preheated oven at Gas Mark 5, 375°F, 190°C for 15 minutes.

3 Beat the filling ingredients together in a bowl.

4 Pour on to the sponge base. Lower the oven temperature to Gas Mark 4, 350°F, 180°C and bake for 30 minutes. Leave to cool, then remove from the tin.

5 For the topping, purée 4oz (125g) strawberries in a blender or food processor until smooth. Sieve to remove seeds. When the cheesecake is cold, spread with the strawberry purée.

6 Slice the remaining strawberries and use to garnish the cheesecake.

PAWPAW AND LYCHEE PAVLOVA

INGREDIENTS

BASE
- 3 egg whites
- 4oz (125g) soft brown sugar
- 2 tbsp (30ml) cornflour

TOPPING
- 1 pawpaw, peeled and finely chopped
- 4oz (125g) natural fromage frais

GARNISH
- 8 lychees, peeled, stoned and halved
- 1 lime, sliced

Illustrated on page 133

This luxurious version of pavlova is made with a low-sugar base. This means it will take longer to cook and is inevitably more sticky. If you prefer the traditional crisper meringue, you will need to add an extra 2oz (50g) of sugar. The fromage frais topping tastes rich but is low in fat. For a plainer alternative, try just fresh fruit or a little natural yogurt.

PREPARATION TIME: 25 mins
COOKING TIME: 1½–1¾ hours
SERVES 4—6

METHOD

1 For the base, combine the egg whites, sugar and cornflour to make the meringue mixture (see right).
2 Spoon into a 6-inch (15cm) round on a baking sheet, lined with greaseproof paper or non-stick baking parchment. Form a hollow in the centre and at the side edges.
3 Bake in a preheated oven at Gas Mark 2, 300°F, 150°C for 1½– 1¾ hours. Cool under a cloth. Then carefully remove the baking paper.
4 Fold the finely chopped pawpaw into the fromage frais and spread over the base.
5 Decorate with the lychees and the slices of lime and serve cold.

MAKING A PAVLOVA

A pavlova is a meringue-based dish, created for the ballet dancer Anna Pavlova when she visited Australia in the 1930s. This version is made with brown sugar and fromage frais, instead of white sugar and cream. The less sugar you use, the softer and stickier the meringue becomes, although it still tastes just as good.

1 Beat 3 egg whites in a large bowl until stiff but not dry.

2 Gradually add 2oz (50g) sugar, whisking all the time. Then whisk in the remaining 2oz (50g) sugar.

3 Fold in the cornflour thoroughly. Spoon the mixture on to a lined baking sheet, making a meringue nest.

SUMMER PUDDING

INGREDIENTS

- 6oz (175g) raspberries
- 4oz (125g) redcurrants
- 6oz (175g) blackcurrants
- 3 fl oz (75ml) red grape juice
- 4oz (125g) mixed grain Swiss bread, without crusts

Illustrated on page 133

This delicious traditional pudding is given a healthy, high-fibre slant here by using a mixed-grain Swiss bread and not overcooking the fruit. Make sure the bread is well moistened by the fruit juice, and push each layer right to the side of the bowl, so that the pudding turns out whole. It works equally well with bilberries, loganberries or tayberries, and is excellent served with natural yogurt, soured cream or smetana.

PREPARATION TIME: 30 mins (plus overnight standing time)

SERVES 4

METHOD

1 Wash all the fruit and string the currants.
2 Place the fruit with the grape juice in a saucepan. Bring to the boil, then leave to cool.
3 Slice the bread thinly. Use one slice to line the base of a 1½ pint (900ml) pudding basin. Spoon over some fruit. Repeat layers of fruit and bread, ending with bread.
4 Put a plate or saucer with weights on the top and leave overnight. Turn out on to a rimmed plate and serve.

ORANGE AND RAISIN GRANOLA

INGREDIENTS

BASE

- 6 oranges (or 4 oranges and 2 pink grapefruit)
- 6oz (175g) seeded raisins

TOPPING

- 8oz (250g) muesli
- 2 tsp (10ml) ground cinnamon
- 2 tsp (10ml) sunflower oil
- 2 tbsp (30ml) clear honey

Illustrated on page 136

Granola is traditionally a baked cereal made from a muesli base and sweetened with oil and malt.

PREPARATION TIME: 30 mins (plus 1 hour soaking time)

COOKING TIME: 20-25 mins

SERVES 4

METHOD

1 Peel and segment the oranges (and grapefruit if using), reserving the juice.
2 Place the segments in a small ovenproof dish. Add the raisins and the orange juice. Leave to soak for 1 hour.
3 For the topping, mix the muesli and cinnamon together. Stir the oil and honey together, then combine with the muesli. Spoon this over the oranges.
4 Bake in a preheated oven at Gas Mark 5, 375°F, 190°C for 20–25 minutes.

PEAR AND ALMOND PUDDING

INGREDIENTS

BASE

- 1½lb (750g) Conference pears
- 2oz (50g) sultanas
- juice and rind of ½ a lemon

TOPPING

- 2oz (50g) wholemeal flour
- 2oz (50g) almonds, chopped
- 1oz (25g) soft brown sugar
- 1 tsp (5ml) ground ginger
- ½ tsp ground cinnamon
- 4 fl oz (125ml) soured cream or smetana

Illustrated on page 136

This light, nutty crumble with its creamy topping complements the taste and texture of the sweet fruit filling and contributes fibre and vitamins.

PREPARATION TIME: 25 mins

COOKING TIME: 15-20 mins

SERVES 4—6

METHOD

1 Slice and core the pears, mix with the sultanas and lemon juice.
2 Fill a 1½ pint (900ml) ovenproof dish with the slices.
3 For the topping, mix together the flour, chopped almonds, sugar, spices and lemon rind. Sprinkle over the fruit.
4 Mix the soured cream or smetana with 1 tbsp (15ml) water. Pour this over the top.
5 Bake in a preheated oven at Gas Mark 5, 375°F, 190°C for 15–20 minutes. Serve the pudding warm.

PLUM CHARLOTTE

INGREDIENTS

■ 8–10 slices of fruit bread
■ 2 tbsp (30ml) blackcurrant jam
■ 1lb (500g) red plums, halved and stoned
■ 1–2 tbsp (15–30ml) clear honey (optional)
■ ¼ tsp ground mixed spice

Illustrated right

Plums are in season in late summer and early autumn. There are many different types: they come with red, black, blue, yellow or green skins; large or small; round or oval; sweet or sour. Plums make wonderful jams, jellies, sauces, purées, mousses and soufflés, but the skin can leave a bitter taste when cooked, so it's often best to peel them. They are also delicious used whole or halved in pies, tarts and flans. As you get used to using less sugar you may not need to sweeten the plums with honey. Some natural yogurt, soured cream or smetana will go well with this dessert.

PREPARATION TIME: 30 mins
COOKING TIME: 50–60 mins
SERVES 4–5

METHOD

1 Cut the crusts off the fruit bread.
2 Spread a little jam on one side of each slice of bread.
3 Lightly grease a 1½ pint (900ml) round ovenproof dish.
4 Cut one slice of bread to fit the base. Then slice the remaining pieces to overlap all around the sides, sticky side outwards. Leave some pieces for the top.
5 Place the plums in a saucepan with the honey and mixed spice and lightly poach for 4 minutes until just softening.
6 Press the plums into the centre of the bread-lined dish. Top with the remaining bread, sticky side down. Cover with foil.
7 Bake in a preheated oven at Gas Mark 5, 375°F, 190°C for 50–60 minutes.
8 Turn out and serve hot with yogurt, soured cream or smetana.

FROM TOP: Pineapple pudding; Orange and raisin granola (see p.135); Pear and almond pudding (see p.135); Plum charlotte

PINEAPPLE PUDDING

INGREDIENTS

- 2oz (50g) margarine
- 1oz (25g) clear honey
- 7oz (200g) skimmed milk soft cheese (quark)
- 1 egg, separated
- 1oz (25g) ground almonds
- 1oz (25g) ground rice
- 1 tsp (5ml) grated orange rind
- 12oz (375g) fresh pineapple

Illustrated left

This light, creamy fruit pudding uses skimmed milk soft cheese, well moistened with almonds and egg. It is an excellent cheese for baking, but its lack of fat can make it dry. To reduce the sugar content, you could make a date purée to use instead of honey.

PREPARATION TIME: 25 mins
COOKING TIME: 50 mins
SERVES 4

METHOD

1 Cream the margarine and honey together in a bowl until light and fluffy.
2 Gradually beat in the skimmed milk soft cheese and egg yolk.
3 Stir in the almonds, ground rice and orange rind. Roughly chop the pineapple and add to the mixture.
4 Beat the egg white until stiff and then fold into the pineapple mixture.
5 Spoon the mixture into a greased 6-inch (15cm) loose-based fluted flan tin. Bake in a preheated oven at Gas Mark 5, 375°F, 190°C for 50 minutes. Leave to cool slightly and then refrigerate. Serve cold with some natural yogurt.

APRICOT AND GOOSEBERRY FLAN

INGREDIENTS

PASTRY
- 4oz (125g) wholemeal flour
- pinch salt
- 4 tsp baking powder
- 2oz (50g) margarine
- 2–3 tsp (30–45ml) water

ALMOND CREAM
- 4oz (125g) ground almonds
- ¼ pint (150ml) water
- ½ tsp ground ginger
- 3–4 drops almond essence
- 1 tbsp (15ml) clear honey (optional)

TOPPING
- 12oz (375g) fresh apricots, halved and stoned
- 3–4oz (75–125g) dessert gooseberries, topped and tailed

Illustrated left

Nut creams are a delicious and healthy alternative to confectioner's custard, particularly as a base for fruit flans. Choose dessert gooseberries for the topping — they are a good source of Vitamin C and dietary fibre.

PREPARATION TIME: 45 mins (plus 30 mins resting time)
COOKING TIME: 35 mins
SERVES 4

METHOD

1 For the pastry, mix together the flour, salt and baking powder in a bowl.
2 Rub in the margarine until the mixture resembles fine breadcrumbs.
3 Sprinkle over the water and make into a firm dough. Leave to rest for 30 minutes.
4 Roll out the dough and use to line a 7-inch (18cm) flan tin. Press in firmly and prick well.
5 Bake in a preheated oven at Gas Mark 6, 400°F, 200°C for 5 minutes.
6 For the almond cream filling, mix all the ingredients together. Sweeten with honey if necessary. Spoon the filling into the flan case.
7 For the topping, place 8oz (250g) apricots on top of the almond cream around the edge of the flan. Fill the centre with gooseberries. Reduce the oven temperature to Gas Mark 5, 375°F, 190°C and bake for 25–30 minutes.
8 Place the remaining apricots in a saucepan with 1 tbsp (15ml) of water. Simmer for 5 minutes. Transfer to a blender or food processor and purée until smooth.
9 When the flan is cooked, carefully spoon over the apricot purée. Serve warm.

FROM LEFT: Orange and apple flan; Apricot and gooseberry flan (see p.138)

ORANGE AND APPLE FLAN

INGREDIENTS

PASTRY
- 4oz (125g) wholemeal flour
- pinch salt
- ½ tsp baking powder
- 2oz (50g) margarine
- 1 tsp (5ml) grated orange rind
- 2–3 tbsp (30–45ml) water

FILLING
- 4 dessert apples, peeled cored and chopped
- 8oz (250g) apricots, halved and stoned
- 2 oranges, peeled and sliced, with juice reserved

GLAZE
- 1 tbsp (15ml) clear honey

Illustrated on page 137

Serve this colourful flan warm with a little natural yogurt, soured cream or smetana.

PREPARATION TIME: 45 mins (plus 30 mins resting time)
COOKING TIME: 30 mins
SERVES 6

METHOD

1 For the pastry, mix together the flour, salt and baking powder in a bowl. Rub in the margarine until the mixture resembles fine breadcrumbs. Add the orange rind and water and mix to a soft dough. Leave to rest for 30 minutes.

2 Roll out and use to line a 7-inch (18cm) flan tin. Press down well and prick the base. Bake in a preheated oven at Gas Mark 6, 400°F, 200°C for 5 minutes.

3 For the filling, place the apples and apricots with the orange juice in a saucepan. Cover and poach for 10 minutes. Purée in a blender or food processor.

4 Fill the flan case with purée. Cover with the slices of orange. Bake for 20–25 minutes. Cool slightly.

5 For the glaze, melt the honey and brush over the fruit. Serve warm.

MAKING PANCAKE CUSHIONS

*P*ancakes are an immensely versatile way of cooking batter. They can be served with a sweet or savoury accompaniment like a vegetable or fruit purée and rolled, folded or layered. They can be easily adapted by using different types of flour, milk, fat and by adding spices or purées.

1 *Fry each pancake in a non-stick pan for 2–3 minutes on each side.*

2 *Spoon on some filling, then fold over the sides and edges to make a cushion.*

3 *Using a greased, ovenproof dish, make two layers of filled pancakes.*

FROM TOP: Peach and nutmeg cushions; Cheese pancakes with apple sauce (see p.140)

PEACH AND NUTMEG CUSHIONS

INGREDIENTS

PANCAKES
- 1 egg
- ½ pint (300ml) skimmed milk
- 4oz (125g) wholemeal flour
- pinch salt
- ¼ tsp grated nutmeg

FILLING
- 4 peaches, skinned, stoned and chopped
- 2 tbsp (30ml) sherry

TOPPING
- ¼ pint (150ml) soured cream or smetana
- ¼ tsp grated nutmeg
- 1 tsp (5ml) soft brown sugar

Illustrated left

This delicious layered pancake pudding is made with an unsweetened peach filling and soured cream or low-fat smetana topping, yet it tastes extremely rich. Smetana tastes like a cross between yogurt and single cream. It is made from skimmed milk and cream, but has only half the calories of cream.

PREPARATION TIME: 60 mins
COOKING TIME: 15 mins
SERVES 4

METHOD

1 For the pancakes, beat the egg and milk together in a blender or food processor. Add the flour, salt and nutmeg and blend again until smooth.

2 Wipe out a frying pan with a little oil. Heat the pan and cook an eighth of the batter (2–3 tbsp/30–45ml), for 2–3 minutes each side. Keep warm while making the remaining 7 pancakes.

3 For the filling, place the peaches in a medium-sized saucepan with the sherry and poach gently for 4–5 minutes, adding a little water if necessary. Spoon some filling into each pancake and fold up to form a small parcel.

4 Layer 4 pancakes on the base of an ovenproof dish. Spread over half the soured cream or smetana. Then make a second layer with the remaining pancakes and cover with the remaining soured cream. Sprinkle on the nutmeg and sugar.

5 Bake in a preheated oven at Gas Mark 4, 350°F, 180°C for 15 minutes.

CHEESE PANCAKES WITH APPLE SAUCE

INGREDIENTS

PANCAKES
■ 2 eggs
■ 7oz (200g) skimmed milk soft cheese (quark)
■ 1 tbsp (15ml) sunflower oil
■ 2oz (50g) wholemeal flour
■ pinch salt

SAUCE
■ 3 dessert apples, cored
■ ½ tsp ground cloves
■ juice of ½ lemon
■ 1 tbsp (15ml) brandy

Illustrated on page 139

The skimmed milk soft cheese in the batter of these small pancakes makes this a nutritious, satisfying pudding — ideal after a light salad.

PREPARATION TIME: 15 mins
COOKING TIME: 30 mins
SERVES 4

METHOD

1 For the pancakes, beat the eggs, add the soft cheese and oil and mix thoroughly, then beat in the flour and a pinch of salt.
2 Wipe out a non-stick frying pan with a little oil. Heat the pan and cook the pancakes, using 1 tbsp (15ml) batter each.
3 For the sauce, place the apples, cloves, lemon juice, brandy and 1–2 tbsp (15–30ml) water in a saucepan. Cover and simmer for 10 minutes until the apples are reduced to a sauce.
4 Serve the pancakes flat with the apple sauce over the top.

FROM TOP: Saucer pancakes; Cherry oaten pancakes

CHERRY OATEN PANCAKES

INGREDIENTS

PANCAKES
■ 1 egg
■ ¼ pint (150ml) skimmed milk
■ ¼ pint (150ml) natural yogurt
■ 2oz (50g) porridge oats
■ 1½oz (40g) wholemeal flour
■ pinch salt

FILLING
■ 1lb (500g) black cherries, stoned
■ juice of 1 large orange
■ 1 tsp (5ml) arrowroot or cornflour

Illustrated left

These pancakes have the texture of drop scones. Although made with skimmed milk they taste creamy because of the smooth texture of the oats. Serve with soured cream, smetana or natural yogurt.

PREPARATION TIME: 15 mins
COOKING TIME: 55 mins
MAKES 8–10 pancakes

METHOD

1 Mix the egg, milk and yogurt together in a blender for 30 seconds.
2 Add the oats, flour and salt. Blend again until smooth. Add enough milk to make a pouring consistency.
3 Wipe out a non-stick frying pan with a little oil. Heat the pan and pour in about an eighth of the batter (2–3 tbsp/30–45ml). Cook on both sides for 2–3 minutes. Keep warm, covered with a clean tea-towel, while cooking the remainder.
4 For the filling, purée 12oz (375g) of the cherries with half of the orange juice in a blender or food processor until smooth.
5 Dissolve the arrowroot or cornflour in a little water and add to the cherry purée. Bring the mixture to the boil and cook until thickened, stirring. Spoon some cherry filling on to each pancake and fold into four. Arrange in a serving dish.
6 Poach the remaining cherries in the orange juice for 5 minutes. Spoon over the pancakes and serve.

SAUCER PANCAKES

INGREDIENTS

PANCAKES
■ 2oz (50g) dried dates, chopped
■ 2oz (50g) margarine
■ 2 eggs, separated
■ 2oz (50g) wholemeal flour

SAUCE
■ ½oz (15g) margarine
■ 4 Conference pears, peeled, cored and finely chopped
■ juice of 1 orange
■ juice of ½ a lemon
■ 1 tsp (5ml) grated orange rind
■ 1 tbsp (15ml) Cointreau (optional)

Illustrated left

This old-fashioned recipe makes thick, spongy pancakes, served warm with a delicious, low-fat pear and orange sauce.
PREPARATION TIME: 20 mins
COOKING TIME: 30 mins
SERVES 4

METHOD

1 For the pancakes, place the dates in a saucepan. Cook gently in a little water for 5–10 minutes, until they make a thick purée.
2 Beat the margarine, date purée, egg yolks and flour together. In a separate bowl, whisk the egg whites until soft, then fold in.
3 Wipe out a non-stick frying pan with a little oil. Heat the pan and pour in a quarter of the batter. Cook on both sides for about 3 minutes. Make 4 thick, saucer-sized pancakes.
4 For the sauce, melt the margarine in a saucepan and gently cook the pears for 2–3 minutes. Add the fruit juices, rind and Cointreau, cover and simmer until soft. Beat to a purée. Spoon some purée on to each pancake, fold in half and serve.

LEMON AND BANANA ROULADE

INGREDIENTS

BASE
■ 3 eggs, separated
■ 1 tbsp (15ml) clear honey
■ rind and juice of 1 lemon
■ 2 bananas, peeled and chopped

FILLING
■ 12oz (375g) raspberries

Illustrated left

This sweet yet sharp-flavoured roulade makes an ideal summer dessert. It is easy to make and yet never fails to impress. The low-calorie base, made with lemon and puréed banana, contrasts well with the raspberry filling and sauce. If you find the mixture will not bind, add a little wholemeal flour, and if raspberries are in short supply, use blackberries, blackcurrants or strawberries instead.
PREPARATION TIME: 40 mins
COOKING TIME: 20 mins
SERVES 6

METHOD

1 Beat the egg yolks and honey together in a bowl. Add the lemon rind and half of the lemon juice.
2 Place the bowl over a pan of steaming water and whisk for 5 minutes until the mixture is very stiff. Remove the pan from the heat and take the bowl off the pan.
3 In a blender or food processor, purée the bananas and remaining lemon juice. Then fold into the egg yolks.
4 In a separate bowl, whisk the egg whites until stiff. Fold into the mixture.
5 Line a Swiss roll tin with greaseproof paper. Spread the roulade mixture evenly over the tin using a palette knife. Bake in a preheated oven at Gas Mark 5, 375°F, 190°C for 15–20 minutes or until lightly browned and firm. Turn out on to a clean cloth covered with greaseproof paper. Carefully peel off the old sheet of greaseproof paper. Cover with a damp cloth and cool.
6 Mash 8oz (250g) raspberries and spread evenly over the roulade. Using the fresh sheet of greaseproof paper to lift and support the roulade, roll it up into a long Swiss roll shape.
7 In a blender, purée the remaining raspberries, sieve and pour a little sauce over the top just before serving.

Lemon and banana roulade

FROM TOP: *Watermelon sorbet; Green grape sorbet*

WATERMELON SORBET

INGREDIENTS

■ 8oz (250g) watermelon flesh
■ 2 tbsp (30ml) sweet white wine or Cointreau
■ juice of ½ an orange
■ 1 tsp (5ml) grated orange rind
■ 1–2 tbsp (15–30ml) clear honey
■ 1–2 egg whites

Illustrated above

This delicately flavoured sorbet is wonderfully refreshing and is best eaten on the day it is made. You may find it more economical to buy a large wedge of watermelon than the entire fruit.
PREPARATION TIME: 20 mins (plus 4–5 hours freezing time)
SERVES 4

METHOD

1 Remove the seeds from the watermelon.
2 In a blender or food processor, purée the watermelon with the wine, orange juice and rind, and the honey.
3 Turn the watermelon mixture into a shallow freezerproof container. Freeze for 3–4 hours.
4 Purée in a blender until smooth.
5 Whisk the egg white until firm but not dry. Fold into the watermelon mixture. Refreeze until just firm.

GREEN GRAPE SORBET

INGREDIENTS

■ 1lb (500g) seedless green grapes
■ 3 tbsp (45ml) clear honey
■ 1 egg white

Illustrated left

Frozen sorbets do need a little sweetening to have flavour. In this recipe the grapes are naturally very sweet and the honey contributes added sweetness.
PREPARATION TIME: 15 mins (plus 4–5 hours freezing time)
SERVES 4

METHOD

1 Purée the grapes in a blender, then sieve for a smooth liquid.
2 Whisk in the honey.
3 Turn the grape mixture into a shallow freezerproof container. Freeze for 3–4 hours.
4 Purée in a blender until smooth.
5 Whisk the egg white until firm. Fold into the grape mixture. Refreeze until the mixture is just firm.

AUTUMN FRUIT SALAD

INGREDIENTS

■ 2 oranges
■ 1 red apple
■ 1 green apple
■ 1 firm pear (preferably William or Packham)

TOPPING

■ 5 fl oz (150ml) natural yogurt
■ 3 tbsp lemon juice
■ 1 tsp (5ml) honey
■ ½ inch (1cm) fresh root ginger, peeled and grated.

GARNISH

■ ½oz (15g) pumpkin seeds

Illustrated right

The secret of a really good fruit salad is to use large chunks of firm fruit and to add plenty of citrus fruit to supply the moisture. Autumn fruits are inexpensive and a low-fat topping keeps the calories down. You can vary the dish by adding other fruits in season. If you select them carefully for their colour and texture, you can achieve a pleasing visual effect.
PREPARATION TIME: 30 mins
SERVES 4

METHOD

1 Peel the oranges. Divide into segments, allowing the juice to drip into a bowl.
2 Chop the apples and pear into chunks, removing the cores.
3 Mix with the orange segments and juice and refrigerate.
4 For the topping, blend the ingredients together in a blender until smooth.
5 Serve the fruit in individual bowls with a spoonful of topping and garnish with pumpkin seeds.

HAZELNUT AND RASPBERRY DESSERT

INGREDIENTS

- 2oz (50g) medium oatmeal
- ½oz (15g) hazelnuts, ground
- ½ tsp ground allspice
- ½ pint (300ml) natural yogurt
- 1–2 tbsp (15–30ml) whisky
- 2 bananas
- 8oz (250g) raspberries

Illustrated right

This deliciously rich pudding is surprisingly healthy — low in fat and high in fibre. The light toasting brings out the flavour of the grain. Other soft fruits in season will work equally well.

PREPARATION TIME: 40 mins (plus chilling time)

SERVES 4

METHOD

1 Mix the oatmeal and hazelnuts together and place on a baking sheet. Roast in a preheated oven at Gas Mark 4, 350°F, 180°C for 8–10 minutes.
2 Add the allspice and allow to cool.
3 Mix the yogurt with the whisky.
4 Slice the bananas, and reserve 4 slices for garnish. Rinse the raspberries.
5 Spoon layers of fruit, grain and yogurt into 4 individual glasses. Finish with a layer of yogurt and garnish with a slice of banana. Refrigerate and serve chilled.

PINEAPPLE BASKET

INGREDIENTS

- 2 small pineapples
- 6oz (175g) cantaloupe or honeydew melon
- 1 mango
- 1 passion fruit
- 1oz (25g) fresh coconut, coarsely grated

TOPPING

- 1oz (25g) fresh coconut
- ½oz (15g) shelled walnuts

Illustrated right

This exotic fruit salad makes a festive and refreshing dessert for a special occasion.

PREPARATION TIME: 40 mins

SERVES 4

METHOD

1 Slice the pineapples in half lengthways and scoop out the inner flesh with a sharp knife.
2 Scoop out the melon flesh into small balls. Peel and slice the mango. Scoop out the flesh of the passion fruit.
3 Mix all the fruit with the grated coconut.
4 Pile the fruit back into the pineapple shells, or serve in bowls.
5 For the topping, grind the coconut and walnuts together in a food processor or nut mill and sprinkle over the fruit.
6 If you like, grill for 2 minutes until the topping is just brown.

FROM TOP: Hazelnut and raspberry dessert; Pineapple basket; Autumn fruit salad

INDEX

Aioli 108
Almond:
  and cauliflower bake 58
  and fennel salad 100
  pudding, pear and 135
  and raspberry soup 17
  and tomato soup 11
  and vegetable paella 62
  wheel 60
Apple:
  orange and apple flan 138
  sauce, cheese pancakes with 140
  spiced purée with 132
Apricot, aubergines stuffed with 56
  and gooseberry flan 137
Artichoke and hazelnut pancakes 81
Artichoke soup, creamed 12
Asparagus soufflé 31
Aubergine:
  and butter bean biryani 53
  charlotte 93
  lasagne, with pepper and mushroom 72
  and mushroom rice 62
  pancakes 81
  rolls, stuffed 38
  stuffed with apricots 56
  stuffing 39
Autumn medley 103
Avocado dressing, spiky beetroot salad and 102
Avocado and lettuce soup 15

Baked Spanish omelette 56
Banana and lemon roulade 141
Banana surprise 126
Banana pancakes, wholemeal 125
Beans:
  baked, traditional 95
  broad, with creamy basil sauce 118
  broad, in pizza pockets 78
  butter, au gratin 50
  butter, and cheese quiche 39
  butter, and haricot chowder 8
  butter, salad with creamy dressing 101
  colourful loaf, with carrot sauce 59
  Dutch bean stamppot 43
  five bean salad 101
  French, and sweetcorn with mint sauce 118
  haricot, with apple and cider 50
  haricot hot-pot, creamy 43
  haricot, and olive bake 36
  haricot, and tomato sauce 52
  red kidney, burgers 37
  red, and olives 50
  red, with soured cream 95
  refritos 118
  sweet and sour 44
  wholemeal pancakes with a spicy bean filling 82
Beans, lentils and grains 22–3
Beetroot:
  red cabbage and 96
  slaw, with orange dressing 105
  spiky salad with avocado dressing 102
Bread, crusty 18
  garlic 18
  sticks (grissini) 17

Cabbage, see Red cabbage
Californian salad with tarragon dressing 107
Cannelloni, making 74
  rice and egg 73

Caraway toast fingers 18
Carrots and dill 118
Carrot sauce, colourful bean loaf with 59
Casseroles:
  cheesy leek and potato 57
  chilli 44
  crunchy, with chick peas 53
  red and orange 48
Cauliflower and almond bake 58
Celeriac, creamed, salad 105
Celery and leeks in sherry 119
Cereals 20–1
Cheese:
  and butter bean quiche 39
  cottage, and fruit platter 130
  cottage, and spinach ravioli 74
  and herb balls 97
  and leek pizza 78
  macaroni, and fennel 69
  Mozzarella and tomato pizza 77
  and parsnip soup with caraway 10
  platter, with fruit and nuts 131
  rusks 18
  and walnut loaf 58
Cheesecake, strawberry 133
Cheesy leek and potato casserole 57
Cherry oaten pancakes 140
Chestnut and mushroom bake 64
Chestnut and orange pâté 26
Chick pea casserole 53
  curried 52
  moussaka 36
  and tomato soup, spiced 9
Chicory:
  crunchy nut salad with 100
  and grapefruit salad 106
  with yogurt hollandaise sauce 92
Chilli casserole 44
Chinese bake with watercress sauce 55
Choux, savoury 31
Classic green salad 106
Classic mayonnaise 109
Coleslaw, traditional, with yogurt and mustard dressing 104
Compote, spiced fruit 131
Consommé:
  with florets 9
  julienne 10
  vermicelli 9
Courgette and lentil gratin 46
Courgettes and peppers, spicy 45
Creamed celeriac salad 105
Creamy haricot hot-pot 43
Crumble, savoury 55
Crumbletop 47
Cucumber and orange soup 15
Cucumber, hot with pistachio nuts 26
Curried chick peas 52
Curried mayonnaise 108
Curry, mixed vegetable 57

Dairy produce 86–7
Dhal 33
Dried fruit 120–1

Eggs florentine 91

Fennel, almond salad and 100
  salad, fruit and 107
  wholemeal macaroni cheese with 69
Flavourings 114–5
French beans and sweetcorn with mint sauce 118
Frosted tomato cocktail 27
Fruit compote, spiced 131
Fruit pancake gateau 125
Fruit risotto 126

Fruit salads:
  autumn 142
  cocktail with curried mayonnaise 102
  fresh date and mango platter 128
  fruit and fennel 107
  fruit and nut 130
  golden fruit 126
  late summer 129
  melon, filled 127
  melon and strawberry, with creamy orange topping 127
  mixed, in spiced yogurt 128
  tropical 130

Garlic bread 18
Garnishes, making 27
Gazpacho 17
Giant wholemeal samosa 48
Gnocchi, herb 92
Gnocchi, walnut 33
Gooseberry flan, apricot and 137
Grape sorbet, green 142
Grapefruit salad, chicory and 106
Grapefruit, chilled, with mint 30
Greek salad 103
Green salad, classic 106
Green split pea soup with coriander 11
Grissini (bread sticks) 17

Haricot bean and olive bake 36
Haricot bean and pepper pizza 77
Haricot beans with apple and cider 50
Haricot beans and tomato sauce 52
Hazelnut loaf with mushroom and pepper sauce 59
Hazelnut and raspberry dessert 143
Hazelnut roast, layered 37
Hazelnut Waldorf salad 100
Herb balls, cheese and 97
Herb mayonnaise 109
Herbs 110–1
Hot cucumber with pistachios 26

Kiwi and passion fruit cake 124
Kiwi fruit, stuffed 129

Lasagne: 21
  aubergine, pepper and mushroom 72
  with bean and tomato sauce 71
  red lentil 68
Layered hazelnut roast 37
Leeks:
  cheese and leek pizza 78
  cheesy leek and potato casserole 57
  in sherry, celery and 119
Lemon and banana roulade 141
Lentils:
  courgette and, gratin 46
  pie, spinach and 41
  quick red 51
  red, lasagne 68
  and vegetable cottage pie 54
Lychee, pawpaw pavlova and 134

Macaroni: 21
  in ginger and tomato sauce 70
  spicy pepper 69
  wholemeal, with fennel 69
Mayonnaises 108–9
Melon, filled 127
  and ginger sorbet 28
  and strawberry salad with creamy orange topping 127
Moussaka, chick pea 36
Mushroom bake, chestnut and 64
Mushroom lasagne with aubergine and pepper 72
Mushroom rice, aubergine and 62
Mushroom salad 104

Mushrooms baked with oregano 96
Mushrooms, stuffed 91

Nut:
  crunchy, salad with chicory 100
  pâté 28
  salad creole 100
Nuts 120–1
Nutty onion flan 40

Olive and tomato ravioli 73
Omelette, baked Spanish 56
Onion, nutty flan 40
Onion pizza tart 96
Onion topping, pizza with 76
Orange and apple flan 138
Orange and chestnut pâté 26
Orange and cucumber soup 15
Orange dressing, beetroot slaw with 105
Orange and raisin granola 135

Paella, almond and vegetable 62
Pancakes, making 80
  artichoke and hazelnut 81
  aubergine 81
  cheese, with apple sauce 140
  cherry oaten 140
  cushions, making 138
  cushions, peach and nutmeg 139
  flan, with pears and red plums 125
  fruit gâteau 125
  saucer 141
  spiced 81
  split pea and potato 83
  wholemeal batter 80
  banana 125
  and spicy bean filling 82
Parsnip soup, cheese and 10
Passion fruit cake, kiwi and 124
Pasta: 20–1
  basic dough 64
  using machine 66
  verde 64
  see also individual types of pasta
Pâté:
  chestnut and orange 26
  nut 28
Pavlova, making a 134
  pawpaw and lychee 134
Peanut and paprika soup 8
Pear and almond pudding 135
Pears with redcurrant sauce 132
Pears and red plums, pancake flan with 125
Pease pudding 93
Pepper pizza, haricot bean and 77
Peppers, lasagne with aubergine, mushrooms and 72
Peppers, spicy courgettes and 45
Peppers, spicy, with macaroni 69
Pineapple basket 143
Pineapple pudding 137
Pistachio nuts, hot cucumber with 26
Pizzas 75–9
Plum charlotte 136
Potatoes:
  casserole, cheesy leek and 57
  Mediterranean 119
  pancakes, split pea and 83
  toppings, making 96
Pumpkin soup, easy 12

Quiche, butter bean and cheese 39

Raspberry and almond soup 17
Ratatouille 44
Ravioli, making 72
  olive and tomato 73
  spinach and cottage cheese 74
Red beans and olives 50
Red beans with soured cream 95

Red cabbage and apple 119
  with beetroot 96
  slaw, with sweet and sour dressing 107
Redcurrant sauce 132
Red kidney bean burgers 37
Red lentil lasagne 68
Red and orange casserole 48
Red split lentils 23
Refritos 118
Rice and egg cannelloni 73
Rice:
  mushroom, with aubergines 62
  sharp, with mild sauce 61
Ricotta roulade 90
Ring mould 61

Salad leaves 84–5
Salads 100–7
Samosa, giant wholemeal 48
Savoury choux 31
Savoury crumble 55
Seeds 120–1
Sharp rice with mild sauce 61
Sorbet, green grape 142
  melon and ginger 28
  watermelon 142
Soups 8–15
Spaghetti 21
  bake, wholemeal 67
  fresh herb 65
  with red lentil sauce 67
  spinach and cheese 66
  wholemeal, with walnut and parsley sauce 65
Spanish salad with tomato dressing 103
Spiced purée with fresh apple 132
Spiced yellow pepper dip 30
Spices 112–3
Spicy courgettes and peppers 45
Spicy pepper macaroni 69
Spinach:
  and cottage cheese ravioli 74
  and cheese spaghetti 66
  and lentil pie 41
  purée, pizza with 75
  with walnuts 63
Split pea and potato pancakes 83
Split pea soup with buttermilk 8
Split pea soup with coriander 11
Strawberry cheesecake 133
Stuffed aubergine rolls 38
Stuffed mushrooms 91
Stuffed peppers 38
Summer pudding 135
Sweet and sour beans 44
Sweetcorn, French beans and, with mint sauce 118

Tagliatelle, making 70
  vegetable, with cheese and tomato sauce 71
Tomato and almond soup 11
  and chick pea soup 9
  and chilli pizza 77
  cocktail, frosted 27
  dressing, Spanish salad with 103
  and ginger sauce, macaroni in 70
  and Mozzarella pizza 77
  and avocado salad with nutmeg dressing 106
  ravioli, olive and 73
Tomatoes, baked 55
Tomatoes and basil with crisp potato topping 95

Vegetable and lentil cottage pie 54

Waldorf salad 101
Walnut and cheese loaf 58
Walnuts, spinach with 63
Watermelon sorbet 142

Yellow pepper dip, spiced 30
Yogurt and tomato soup 15